The Enviable Lifestyle:

Creating a Successful
Massage Therapy Business

Principle-Based Marketing
for Creating a Thriving Massage Therapy Practice

The Enviable Lifestyle:

Creating a Successful Massage Therapy Business

Bill Norman, LMBT NC1601
Shelley Johnson, LMBT NC1619

The Enviable Lifestyle Series

To massage therapists everywhere, who want to be successful business owners. We wish you the best of luck. Work hard on your business, continue to work hard on your self, stay the course and enjoy the journey.

"There is nothing more powerful than an idea whose time has come."

~ DR. WAYNE W. DYER

THE ENVIABLE LIFESTYLE SERIES

Table of Contents

Acknowledgements

We have many, many people to thank for helping to bring this book to life. Invariably we will miss some names, but we will never forget the actual people or their invaluable contribution.

First, for our massage education and passage into the profession; we want to thank the co-directors of Body Therapy Institute, Rick Rosen and Carey Smith. They consistently hold their program at the highest level of professionalism; instilling in their students an altruistic view of the somatic impact massage can have on the lives of people we are honored to touch and at the same time giving their students a realistic view of what is required to be successful in this profession.

Second, for our financial success; we want to thank our mentor, our CFO, and our dear friend Roy Hill. In the world of small business, he graced us with a complete and accurate balance sheet that most large corporations only hope for; numbers, totals, summations, percentages to sales, cost per session, and profit margins. He continues to be one of our biggest supporters.

Third, to all the individuals that helped us along the way, most importantly our clients, but also the folks that read the book in its various iterations and added a part to the final product with timely and insightful comments. They included Norm Lindsay, Heather McIver, Marty Johnson, Mack Arrington, Natalie Hyde, Ross Cox, just to name a few. And, to the "other author", Brian Ellis...for his untold hours of working, listening, taping and transcribing our words...thank you.

And last but never least, this book could not have been written without the love, support, understanding and encouragement of our children, Lesley and Andrew. Oh, tiny cat, where are we going for our next vacation?

Introduction

In response to the sincere inquiries from many massage therapists who have come to us over the last several years wanting to understand what is necessary to create and sustain a successful massage therapy practice, we have found ourselves wishing to communicate a message of positive hope and encouragement based upon our actual experiences as therapists and business owners. This book is a labor of love from our hearts and our heads. As you will discover in the following chapters, you will need both in order to succeed in your practice.

We came to massage therapy, as a profession, out of a desire to share the tremendous rewards we both had discovered through our own experiences, but we brought with us backgrounds from the world of business. From the very beginning, we understood our place in the community was as a business entity. That meant we had to operate our practice just like any other business owner, even though this occupation has some very unique characteristics that often run counter to the traditional corporate world. We also realize many people who choose massage therapy do so because the majority of the typical business community does not allow or respond well to the kind of warmth and caring associated with our industry. But, being compassionate must be balanced with a firm commitment to be business-minded and dedicated to the success of your practice.

We started our practice with a broad knowledge of sound business practices based on our corporate careers; but that doesn't mean anyone who lacks this information is destined to fail. Even with our background, we made mistakes, had days of frustration, and wondered if we had made the correct decision. Success isn't something that comes to the privileged few like an inheritance. It takes work—hard work and dedication to the idea that, first and most importantly, a massage therapy practice is a business operation. That doesn't take anything away from the personal attributes you bring to each client, but it does mean you have to see what you're doing as an enterprise in which you must create the environment and the mechanics for reaching and exceeding your own individual goals.

> *Success, isn't something that comes to the privileged few like an inheritance. It takes work—hard work and dedication.*

Our own success didn't materialize overnight. We didn't wake up one morning and tell each other, "Hey, look we made it." We did, however, get up each day believing no one was going to deliver a thriving practice to our doorstep like the morning paper, we have to create what we want. And we get up each day still with the same continuing philosophy that whether or not we are successful depends largely on our willingness to adhere to the principles which have gotten us to this point. We realized what we were doing to achieve our goals was not exclusive to our own situation. When other massage therapists ask what they need to do to make their practices work, we tell them the same things we continue to tell ourselves. As more and more therapists began to ask us for advice, we discovered how little information was actually available that was specific to *building* a sustainable massage therapy business. What is out there concentrates on start-up issues, and while it is vital to know how to create effective business cards and brochures, what is more relevant and important is to understand how to utilize your unique circumstances as an individual to attract and keep clients, create and grow yourself as a business owner, align yourself with other successful businesses and, finally, how to make the sales which are critical to the financial success of your business.

This book is about the next step, about developing an individual strategy for longevity. The nine Principles are purposefully broad because each massage therapist potentially brings something slightly different to his or her practice. Our objective was not to write a step-by-step manual any massage therapist could follow exactly and come out on the other side with a thriving practice. With all our differences and unique circumstances that would not be possible anyway. The book is designed to encourage you think about big ideas and how those overarching concepts can assist you in cultivating your own ideal practice. We've included many examples from our own experience of how the Principles have worked for us, and we're confident you will find how beneficially they can be for you too. In the end, success in business has nothing to do with luck or destiny; it has everything to do with dedication, steadfastness, commitment, and belief in your self. We sincerely believe every massage therapist is capable of creating a uniquely satisfying practice—however it is personally defined. Use these Principles as a road map for charting your individual journey, and you will discover, as we have, that a career in massage therapy really does afford you the enviable lifestyle most people never achieve.

> *In the end, success in business has nothing to do with luck or destiny; it has everything to do with dedication, steadfastness, commitment, and belief in your self.*

Bill Norman and Shelley Johnson-Norman

Section I

OK, I've Graduated, Now What?

Chapter 1

Massage Therapy— An Enviable Lifestyle

*"You'll recognize your own path when you come upon it,
because you will suddenly have all the
energy and imagination you will ever need."*

~ Jerry Giles

Regardless of your background or motivation for entering the field of massage therapy, you most likely have an idea of what kind of lifestyle you want. For some of you, the lifestyle represents the freedom and excitement of self-employment, of being your own boss. For others, it means the allure (and misconception) of charging and bringing home a substantial hourly rate, and for others, it simply stands for a career in which you can exercise your desire to help and enrich people's lives. Whatever the benefits you hope to achieve by owning your own massage therapy practice, the one common factor is the opportunity to create an environment where your work life and your personal life converge daily. Few other professions offer such a powerful benefit.

When we talk about the enviable lifestyle of a massage therapist, we mean you have the ability, unlike many other occupations, to be self-directed and uncompromising in your business decisions. For instance, you can work the hours you want, dress the way you want, provide your service to the clients you want, and most importantly, you can infuse your individual personality into everything your practice represents. Massage therapists have the opportunity to be as unique as fits their styles, but many recently licensed therapists envision one lifestyle, surrounded with success and an extensive, and loyal, clientele while running their practices in a manner that will never allow them to reach that status.

We believe wholeheartedly every massage therapist can attain success, despite the influx of thousands of new massage therapists into the marketplace, and you all can achieve the lifestyle you want. Our interpretation is a holistic, organic one. We have created our own lifestyle by concentrating on who we are as individuals and how those images reflect in our business and by understanding and providing for the needs of our clients. We have a beautiful situation, in which we feel satisfied and comfortable, both financially, but most importantly emotionally. And that is where we differ from many descriptions of the wonderful lifestyle of a small business owner.

When we began our practice, we came from the corporate world. We chose to make an enormous alteration in our lives and the lives of our children. We were, as we describe it, **Career Changers**, as many of you no doubt are. We left the corporate business community, which afforded us steady salaries, employee benefits, and job security; to embark on a new path. The financial material benefits the corporate world championed no longer held the same value. When we started our business, we lowered our financial expectations because there was no safety net, no fall-back. We put all our chips on the table and told ourselves we would make it work one way or another. There was no going back. As our poker-playing son, Andrew, would say, we were "all-in."

What we realized in narrowing our definition of financial success to reflect a different standard was we gained a significant broadening of our emotional expectations. What we perceived made us happy was the fact that we didn't have to fit the mold of a company manual in order to do our jobs and make a living. In fact, it became less about *"making a living,"* in terms of a compartmentalized section of our day, and more about *"being present and living the life we were making"* based on our personal interests and desires. That is the essential difference between massage therapy and other occupations. We were bringing our true personalities out of the realm of our private lives and into our office. The lifestyle we're talking about focuses on the whole person. It's about who you are outside the office and merging it into how you create your practice. It's not a "business" you come to each day; you incorporate your particular spirit into the environment your practice becomes. The perfect practice is built on who you are, and because it is of your own creation, the joy and satisfaction will spread beyond the walls of your office and make *the lifestyle* that much more attractive to you. You aren't just happy at work or just happy at home; you're sustained by the embodiment of a single purpose and vision of what emotional satisfaction means throughout and across your life.

In essence, you redefine your rewards. Before we became massage therapists, the rewards of our jobs were mostly monetary. Our salaries, and our dutiful adherence to company policy, allowed us to live a certain way, though that increasingly conflicted with how we defined happiness. A business in massage therapy is more than trading dollars for services. It's about fulfilling a desire to express your self one way all the time—at home and at work. This is not to say there isn't a high level of professionalism. It simply means if you happen to be a soft-spoken, quiet person, you don't have to pretend to be gregarious to satisfy a job description. Likewise, if you are extremely social and talkative, you don't have to create a practice based on reserved, political correctness. Office protocol is solely defined by you and for the benefit of you and your clients. Because we're all different, each of our practices will be different, and we will attract, and be attracted to, different kinds of potential clients (more on this later.) Living and creating an environment where you can express your personality all the time gives you the foundations on which to build a successful, thriving practice.

The advice throughout this book is intended to help you recognize opportunities you may have overlooked or discarded to build your business. If you can easily relate to the concept of the uncompromising or self-directed lifestyle, you have a much greater chance of success over the long-term. Trying to build your practice based on principles in which you don't believe strongly will ultimately lead to a marginal rate of success— both emotionally and financially. Most massage therapists we talk to have no problem defining and executing an office environment which reflects who they are. The question we're most frequently asked is: How do I make it work? No matter where you are in life or what your ultimate goals are, you have to bring clients into your office in order to succeed. Your perfect work/life balance won't mean much when you can't pay your bills. The stumbling block for many of you is a misunderstanding of what must be done to reach those goals. In working with current students, recent graduates, and even established therapists, we've found there is a disconnect between their ideas of freedom, flexibility, and satisfaction and the manner by which they plan to get there.

People often mistake our own success as having developed out of a desire to engage in that flexibility. They see the success we've had and believe it happened as a result of having a business card, a phone number, and a few clients while we spent the rest of our time basking in the luxury of having free time. They think we somehow transformed that mentality into the busy practice we have today. We never viewed our business as simply an opportunity to enjoy a casual day of providing massage to a couple of clients. There is, of course, nothing wrong with a massage therapist who wants to do this. If you are achieving the goals you've set for yourself, then you are no less successful than someone who has a fully booked appointment book every week, rain or shine.

We call these therapists who only want to work within specific time and financial boundaries **Discretionary Income-Makers**. They are typically motivated by a desire to assist with their family's financial stability but not be the sole provider. Their lifestyle choice is more about enjoying the flexibility of their schedules while making money for special purchases. When this method is part of the predetermined plan and you can achieve it, then we count it as a success. We want to stress that we don't disparage massage therapists who have achieved their goals by this manner. We only distinguish it from the lifestyle of a growing, full-time practice. Still, even this kind of massage therapist must justify the expenses of the business by having paying clients. Employing some of the strategies in this book can increase your client base while allowing you to remain in control of how and when you run your practice.

Even Discretionary Income-Makers can be uncompromising, self-directed and fulfilled by the lifestyle they've chosen.

While Career Changers and Discretionary Income-Makers tend to be middle-aged, Young Graduates typically have chosen massage therapy as their first career as an adult. This group also tends to be more idealistic when it comes to thinking they can achieve long-term success by the sheer nature of being a massage therapist. As we said before, we didn't reach our current level of success by believing the clients would come through the door by themselves. Young Graduates see the opportunities of owning their own practices as a way to do something they like to do without the pressures and demands of a traditional occupation. Here again, the motivations for becoming a massage therapist are as varied as the individuals, and we don't advocate one type of motivation over another. We're merely concerned with showing massage therapists, from any of these categories, how to find success and fulfillment through proven strategies.

Whether you're a **Career Changer**, a **Discretionary Income-Maker**, or a **Young Graduate**, the uncompromising, self-directed lifestyle is available to you. The opportunity to be real and to find clients who positively respond and react to your authenticity is the ultimate success. We define that success as achieving happiness not affluence, and while a self-sustaining practice is necessary (especially if it is your sole source of income,) it is the refining of the definition that is all-important. Success for us in the beginning was realizing the minimum requirement to reach our goal. At first, that goal was flat-out to pay our bills. We discovered what we absolutely had to do for that to happen. As our practice grew, our goals expanded, but we always defined success by how many massages we needed to perform in order to achieve that goal—financially and emotionally.

We went from a mentality of being an employee, getting a salary and basing our decisions on that monthly allotment to; owning a business with no promised salary and concentrating on the direct correlation between what we financially wanted and needed to achieve and how many massages it would take to accomplish that goal. We took our goal and divided it by our hourly rate to determine the number of massages it would take to meet that goal. So, if you want to make $50,000, and you charge $60 per hour, you would need to do approximately 833 massages for the year, or 16 massages a week, PLUS however many massages it takes to cover your business expenses. While our goals have changed over the years, we still evaluate our success by whether or not we've met the requirements necessary to attain that goal. Anything above and beyond that minimum is simply extra. For every one of you, success will be defined individually, and when those goals are met, they will have come about through your personal and deliberate choices.

> *We went from a mentality of being a former employee, receiving a salary and basing our personal financial decisions on that monthly allotment to; owning a business with no promised salary and concentrating on the direct correlation between what we financially wanted and needed to achieve and how many massages it would take to accomplish that goal.*

Obviously, we believe our lifestyle is fantastic for us, but it didn't come about without work. We made mistakes along the way, and we got discouraged sometimes, but we kept in front of us the notion that massage therapy was what we wanted to do and what made us happy. We were committed to success because we recognized this as the very best option for enjoying an uncompromising and self-directed lifestyle outside of massage. If you're reading this book, you've probably made some commitment to pursuing a career in massage therapy. We would be less than realistic if we suggested all massage therapists achieve the benefits and rewards we're talking about. Hundreds of therapists struggle day-in and day-out with the question of how to attract clients, and it doesn't matter how you came to massage. You can be a **Career Changer**, a **Discretionary Income-Maker**, a **Young Graduate**, or a separate category you place yourself in—and still fail. We don't want that to happen. We want you to reach the goals you set for yourself, and the goal of this book is to provide you with principle-based marketing ideas for accomplishing that objective.

We would never have made it to the place we are today if we hadn't set goals and worked out the methods by which we would achieve them. If you are a **Career Changer**, you probably have taken this route because previous jobs did not allow you to be yourself. Plus, succeeding as a massage therapist means you never have to go back to the corporate world. Likewise, the **Discretionary Income-Maker** must be able to cover the expenses of the business and not lose money, even if the ultimate goal is to work only for a specific number of clients. For the **Young Graduate**, while potentially having more possibilities for career changes in the future, choosing this field in the first place was about succeeding. Anyone can work for a salon or a spa for only two days a week, and that's okay, but the purpose of this book is for you to be able to implement specific marketing tools and techniques (that fit your style and plan) to sustain and grow your own independent practice.

Success is absolutely possible with a little know-how and a lot of determination. You made it through massage school for goodness sake! While our intention is not to present this material like a textbook, consider yourself beginning a study of success. The principles are proven, and they work, but not everything we've included will appeal to you, and that's perfectly fine. Explore and use them as stepping stones for your own ideas. We don't pretend to have the only successful methods. We're merely suggesting that by employing a variety of these marketing principles in a consistent way, you are much more likely to reach the goals you've defined for being successful. Reaching those goals gives you a sense of accomplishment, and that feeling helps perpetuate your lifestyle. It is in the opportunity to live each day without compromising who you are while you build a business of your own creation that is the ultimate success story. Who wouldn't envy that? Now, let's get started.

Chapter 1

Summary and Things to Consider

Do you consider yourself to be a career changer? Do you consider yourself a discretionary income-maker or a young graduate? Understanding this helps you to begin to define what your goals and objectives are for being a massage therapist. Do you need a full income? Do you plan to have a professional office setting?

Take your estimated financial goal (including salary and office expenses); divide it by the hourly rate you plan to charge and you are left with the number of massages you will need to do in order to meet that goal.

$$ Yearly Goal ÷ $$ Hour Massage Rate = Number of Massages

Chapter 2

Heart, Hands...and a Brain: Our

Philosophy of Success

"And the stories you'll find here reveal something that is extremely simple but awe-inspiringly powerful - that people want to do the right thing, they want to create and offer quality things, they want to do good in the world, and if you give them the opportunity and the resources to do so, they will shine. Here's to all the stories that are yet to be told."

~ Jim Alling, President, Starbucks U.S. Business

Before we begin detailing the marketing principles for building your business, we need to explain our philosophy for success in massage therapy. Your practice won't succeed or fail in a vacuum, and simply employing a few marketing strategies may entice a client or two in the short-term, but changing your mindset and gaining an understanding and application of these underlying principles of marketing a private practice will ultimately provide you long-range success. There are three components to our philosophy:

1) The first component is the heart. Passion must be present to create a massage practice. This idea almost goes without saying, of course, because most people who go into massage therapy have a sufficient degree of passion about the occupation. Heart is essential as far as desire goes, but it, first and foremost, represents compassion. No matter what the circumstances, you must always be aware of the importance of being honestly compassionate for the needs of your clients. Heart is why most people choose massage therapy in the first place. They recognized the benefit because they received it themselves and decided they wanted to give that gift to others. If you're wondering how any of this relates to building your practice, just stay with us, you'll see how it all fits perfectly together.

2) The second component of our philosophical triangle is the hands. The hands are the piece of education you've received. They represent the skills you've acquired. Without hands, you couldn't be a massage therapist. The mastery of the various techniques you employ gives you the right to designate yourself a massage therapist, instead of, say, an auto body mechanic or a swimming pool installer. While all three of these components are critical to success, the hands are the least important for a thriving practice. What?! Did you stake your success on your ability to give massage *better* than others? Were you at the top of your class, receiving glowing commendations from your instructors? We're not suggesting

one's skills aren't necessary nor are we proposing all massage therapists are created equal, but the hands are a prerequisite. You had to learn how to conduct a Swedish massage or a myofascial release massage before you could offer it to clients.

But, here's the problem with expert skills. If you don't have any clients, it doesn't matter how many A's you received during your certification program. Likewise, you can have all the passion and desire to help people and never get your practice off the ground. Why? You have to use your head. Let us repeat this...

3) The third component of this philosophical triangle is the head. To create a successful massage therapy practice, you must use your brain to continue to achieve the goals of your passion and your skills. Without being business-minded and intellectual about your business, you'll lose heart, give up, and the skills you so diligently learned will be for nothing. As long as your heart continues to tell you massage therapy is what you've chosen to do, then you can move forward.

> *To create a successful massage therapy practice, you must use your brain to continue to achieve the goals of your passion (heart) and your skills (hands).*

Massage therapists tell us all the time how strongly they feel about massage, and most of them are undeniably knowledgeable as far as the skills go. Most of them believe they've used their brains to learn the material necessary for them to practice, but that's not what we're talking about, we're talking about applying knowledge for success. The brain component of business is something you either have, or you get it from someone else. Basically, you either intuitively recognize what it takes to make your practice a success, or you seek the advice of others who have been successful before you. We're not suggesting you can't figure it out on your own. We're simply saying if you're going to create your practice into a busy, thriving business, you must look at it from all three angles.

There's no getting around the fact that a massage therapy practice is a business. You can want to help and nurture people and still treat what you do as a business. And as such, it means you must attract and retain clients. Many people mistake skills for success. The wider the range of your skill sets, the better chances you have to be successful. Not true. Being trained in a variety of techniques does afford you a bigger tool belt, but unless you have someone to work on, it doesn't really help you. Massage therapists also confuse retaining clients with attracting them, and the techniques for each are different. Your unique personality is very important in how strongly a client is initially attracted to you, and the connection between therapist and client is a critical component of retention. But, until that relationship is established, your phone number on a business card or in the phone book doesn't convey the message that you are a particular client's ideal therapist. That only happens <u>after</u> you give them massage.

> *Your unique personality is very important in how strongly a client is initially attracted to you, and the connection between therapist and client is a critical component of retention.*

We graduated from massage school in August, and the following January, we had a total of three (3) clients for the month, three. A total revenue of $180 for the month to pay our office rent, our mortgage, utilities, phone, advertising, food..and 2 growing teenagers with their expectations. We had very few business relationships established, and the public didn't know our name. Plus, we were competing with many of our graduating class, as well as established therapists in the area. If we had simply relied on our heart and our hands to bring in clients, we would have failed miserably. We realized quickly we had to use our heads to let prospective clients know who we were, where we were, what we did, and what made us different. We had to think fast and act fast. It is this triangular principle of the heart, hands, and brain that leads to success. No matter how you look at it, you limit your chances for success when you're missing any one of the three components.

The Importance of a Business Plan

One of the first exercises for your brain is to create a business plan. Many schools today are requiring students to write a business plan as part of the curriculum. From our experience, this assignment in the classroom is often misunderstood and misguided. In main-stream business situations, a business plan is the tool a business owner uses to prove to a financial institution his or her company has the strength and stability on which to merit receiving a loan. In massage therapy, the only true assets you have are your hands, so if you expect to use your "A+" business plan from massage school to secure funding for your new practice, it probably won't happen, but none-the-less your goals are still achievable. Regardless of your previous background before massage therapy, the significance of the business plan is difficult for many interested in massage therapy to recognize. It is essential to defining your level of success.

A business plan is more realistically a method for thinking about and fine tuning how you want your practice to look, how you want it to feel, what message you want to convey. It is also a practical way for you to itemize what it will cost you, in actual dollars, to run this business. While you can find many excellent reference guides for creating a business plan, we want you to understand a broader purpose for utilizing it in your daily practice. The business plan forces you to look at your wants, needs, and goals to find the path that fits your practice and lifestyle. It isn't a static document to be filed away with all your other school papers upon graduating. It's not just a template you fill out with numbers representing abstract ideas. A business plan is about searching your soul and discovering, in writing, what you need to do to achieve the dream of undeniable happiness. So, we see the business plan as both practical and emotional. Your business plan should be a living document! To be revised overtime as the practice grows and changes. Without a business plan, you have no written idea of where you're starting from or where you're going.

> *A business plan is about searching your soul and discovering, in writing, what you need to do to achieve the dream of undeniable happiness.*

Your business plan should tell you how much your rent will be each month and how much a table costs and what all your other expenses will be, but much more importantly, it helps you consciously and intellectually see your practice as a developing, dynamic entity. When you complete the assignment in school, a business plan has no application. It is merely another task you accomplished for a grade. Consider this analogy. You study shiatsu as part of your curriculum. You learn all the components of this technique, and you even practice on fellow classmates. You get an "A" for the class. When you graduate and start your practice, you could potentially never use shiatsu again in your life. First, you forget the value it can have in specific cases, and then you forget how to perform the technique at all. The same often happens with the business plan. If it is merely another "skill" you learn during the course of your education, not employing it will reduce your ability to use that skill in the future. It is a map to your happiness and success through practical "brain" work, emotional "heart" work, and tactile "hand" work. It completes the three-pronged approach to turning your "idea" of a successful massage therapy practice into a reality.

Convergence and the Balancing Act

So, what happens after you've accepted the need for these three facets of success? Heart, hands and brain. How do you make them converge? Just as the mind, body, and spirit are continually revolving in and through each other, the heart, hands, and the brain are perpetually flowing back and forth among themselves. It's a combination of doing what you want to do (the heart and hands) and making it happen through conscious decision-making (the brain.) When we step into the office to be with a client, we're thinking about him/her at that moment, but we're also thinking about the potential of that person five years from now. What we do and say with that client today affects the chances of that client returning. So, we are passionately involved and technically precise, but it's all about going that extra step to use your brain to see your clients and your whole practice as a business depending exclusively on you for success.

We call this convergence practicing *unconditional positive regard*. From the moment you step into the room, you must be present and focused on the client. It is the heart, hands, and the brain working in conjunction to hear what the client needs and then technically provide the solution. From a business standpoint, your clients have to recognize you are solely focused on them throughout the session. That is, in effect, what brings them back. Discounts, loyalty programs, and specials are all useful, but when the client realizes—and feels—they are all you care about for "their" specific hour, you increase your chances for repeat business exponentially.

When you can concentrate both on what clients need and want, as well as what keeps them coming back, you have a much better idea of how well you are doing. It comes to down to fulfilling the need. It's more than nurturing (heart and hands.) The brain must be active in the process. Thinking about your clients from an intellectual standpoint isn't cold and calculating. It's really about recognizing how everyone can benefit. Regardless of the frequency of visits, you must always provide the client with what they need at that particular time. You need to ask yourself: Am I fulfilling that particular clients' need each and every time? It has to be a conscious thought process, or you'll get tired of working on the same person and lapse into "doing your dance" without analyzing what the client needs at each individual session. What the client flees and what you do with your hands (your intentions) are of equal importance. This exchange creates the "bridge of trust" between client and therapist.

In massage and in much of alternative health practice, balance is a key issue. You also need to achieve a balance between your heart, hands, and brain. Too much heart with not enough brain can create financial gaps when unexpected circumstances arise and clients stop making appointments. On the other hand, too much brain and not enough heart can wear you out when you realize you're spending so much time attracting new clients and providing massage for them that you no longer can enjoy yourself. Additionally, if all you do is acquire skills and add new techniques to your services, you run the risk of having no clients and giving up on your desire to be a massage therapist altogether.

This philosophy of the heart, hands, and a brain is like the food pyramid. You can't survive on heavy cream alone, but if used sparingly, it adds a beneficial dimension to your overall experience. So, you must balance your sense of nurturing and compassionate care and your technical expertise with productive intelligent marketing and overall business practices. When you achieve this equilibrium, you will feel better and more satisfied about your practice, and your clients will respond positively as well. Not only will they connect with you as a therapist, they will react well to your marketing and gain respect for your business practices.

Let us explain how we do this in our own practice. When a client schedules a massage, we realize we must employ unconditional positive regard from the moment the client walks into our office. The actual session is about listening and responding to the needs the client expresses, but the session isn't just the time behind the door. How we treat them both before and after the session is as important to the overall experience as the one-hour massage. When a massage is completed and the client is dressed again, we immediately return to that person to follow through. It is, by far, the best time to position ourselves for the next massage appointment. This cannot be a hard sell, because while the physical action of giving massage is finite and specific for you as the therapist, it is very much more than that for the client.

The physical and emotional realities of the experience go beyond the table, and many of our clients like to talk about how they feel. Their willingness to express themselves gives us a clearer idea of whether we fulfilled their needs. By allowing enough time between sessions for this conversation to take place, at the client's choosing, we reinforce the positive experience. Trying too hard to garner compliments or reassurance of a successful massage can turn people away, and you don't want to make someone feel uncomfortable, especially following an experience designed to help them relax. We are attuned to the whole experience-and the benefit- for both the client and ourselves. When we use unconditional positive regard, and we balance our heart, hands, and brain, our clients receive the best possible experience we can offer, and we maintain a positive sense of who we are and where our practice is going.

By the time you finish massage school, your heart and hands are a given. You have the passion, and you have the skills, but don't stop there. Now, you must invest your time, energy, and resources into developing the mental aspect of your business. Most massage therapists fail for this very reason. They just don't use their brains. While that may sound harsh and callous, you always have to keep in mind you are running a business, and though "feeling" is a critical component to massage, the balance occurs when your brain sometimes takes the lead and makes the decision over the heart. This is a learned business skill.

As we mentioned earlier, a business plan is a very important stepping stone for defining your goals and plans for the practice you want to create, so if you don't have one – stop right now and start creating one. Once you have that, marketing your business is the next step in achieving success. In the next chapter, we'll discuss some of the common myths and misconceptions massage therapists have about marketing and why this gets them in trouble. Then, in the following chapters, we'll show you some marketing principles—not tips—for generating long-term success in your practice and why they work.

Chapter 2

Summary and Things to Consider

- Create a Business Plan - there are numerous templates for creating a business plan that can be found online or in books. (We suggest reading Business Mastery by Cherie Sohnen-Moe.) To help with this exercise, answer the following questions:

  - How do you want your practice to look?

  - How do you want your practice to feel?

  - What message do you want to convey by the look and feel of your practice?

  - Itemize your expenses.

  - Estimate your required salary.

  - Determine and Define what all will you need to run your business.

- Determine ahead of time what to say to a client that will affect the chances of her returning.

- Begin to understand that having a successful massage practice is "more than the hour".

Chapter 3

Ten Myths About A Massage Therapy Practice

"The major value in life is not what you get.
The major value in life is what you become."

~ Jim Rohn

No matter where you attended massage school or where you graduated in your class, the academic setting isn't equipped to represent a massage therapy practice in the real world. It isn't designed for that purpose. With a finite number of hours in which to teach you the science of the body and the various methodologies of massage, schools guide you through the process of mastering technique and anatomy. They teach where to apply pressure, <u>not</u> where to find clients. They teach how to be a massage therapist, <u>not</u> how to be a businessperson. So, naturally, you develop your own conclusions about what life will be like "on the outside." Misconceptions about being a massage therapist abound among the newly graduated. We know because we had several assumptions ourselves. They turned out to be as wrong for us as they will be for you.

Whether you're just starting out on your own or you've been in practice for years struggling to get to the next level, dispelling these myths as soon as possible will benefit your practice. Many times massage therapists get into the real world and begin practicing and discover it's not quite what they had expected. While you may realize your preconceived ideas aren't exactly coming true, it is often hard to let go of them fully. In the back of your mind, you still want to hold up the ideas as the truth, even when believing them doesn't provide you with the results they supposedly should. In a great many cases, the school you went to couldn't clarify the misconceptions for you before they became engrained into your ideals, so let's take a look at the ten biggest misconceptions about a massage therapy practice.

Myth 1:

Because I am a massage therapist,

clients will automatically call.

This first myth is the most widespread of all, and it's the one more massage therapists continue to believe well into their careers. The basic premise is they associate what they are offering as completely satisfying and wonderful, so because there's no downside to receiving massage, people will line up at the door. We talk to massage therapists all the time who can't understand why people aren't calling them once they open their practices. Unfortunately, attracting clients doesn't have anything to do with setting up your table and getting a business card.

The interest and personal satisfaction you may have in being a massage therapist doesn't automatically transfer to the general populace. Consider for a minute how often you thought about massage before you started to school. Fifty percent (50%) of massage therapy students have never received a massage prior to starting massage school. This is such a common thread that most massage therapy programs have to require students to get massage for experience. Forty percent (40%) of the remaining half, have only received one or two. It's only a small minority of students who received regular massage prior to entering a program. The point is, generally speaking, people who aren't currently working with a therapist, rarely think about massage at all; much less think of a specific individual who has recently hung out a sign for business.

This myth is perpetuated by your association with other massage therapy students. In school, everyone eats, drinks, and sleeps massage. Your peers are enthusiastic, interested, and motivated by their own ambitions to be massage therapists. The people who may become your clients don't have the same sense of ecstatic emotion. Don't expect anyone to call you up on your brand new phone number and say, "I'm so glad you are finally practicing. When can I come?"

> *Unfortunately, attracting clients doesn't have anything to do with setting up your table and getting a business card.*

While it may sound silly presented in this fashion, many massage therapists believe clients will come to them <u>because</u> they are currently open for business, not because they marketed themselves to attract clients. Success doesn't come because you have a license; it comes because you actively attracted your clientele. While massage is a very beautiful thing in itself, don't mistake the intrinsic benefits of massage and your profession as a massage therapist as a kind of client magnet by which they will somehow gravitate to your table.

Myth 2:

I'm going to make $60-70 per hour.

While there are relatively few people who go into massage therapy for enormous riches, many massage therapists have a misconception about how much of their fees they will ultimately bring home. Collecting $65 per hour doesn't translate into net revenue or money in your pocket, and basing your income on gross profits can quickly lead to financial challenges. There are many expenses that cut into that $65 fee for a massage. First and foremost, you are responsible for paying your own taxes. Also, many massage therapists have a monthly rent to pay for office space, and this is usually the biggest continual expenditure. There are other costs to factor in as well. You have to have a table, linens, oils, phone, music and other supplies. You may have to pay for your own health insurance. There are association dues, professional liability insurance, continuing education courses, magazine subscriptions, and most importantly, marketing costs.

In school, you concentrate on your course work and utilize the equipment provided by the facility, but once that certificate is in your hand, it is up to you exclusively to balance the money coming in and the money going out. It's sometimes difficult to make a direct correlation between the fees you collect and the business bills you must pay. It's more exciting to think about the $195 you made from three clients, but if you focus too much of your attention on multiplying your hourly rate by the number of clients you have, you'll have an inaccurate assessment of your financial stability. That's why it is vitally important to maximize the practical side of your business plan.

> *Collecting $65 per hour doesn't translate into net revenue or money in your pocket, and basing your income on gross profits can quickly lead to financial challenges.*

As we mentioned before, the business plan forces you to account for all the expenses you'll incur all the way to establishing your practice. What percentage of your hourly rate must go to office rent or supplies or marketing? Knowing what your goals are helps you determine how you proceed. If your goal is to bring home $2000 a month, that doesn't mean you only need to conduct thirty massages at $65 each. It means you have to determine how much you have to make to cover all your business expenses and still have $2000 left over when all the business bills are paid. So, if you have $750 in business expenses, you would add that amount to the $2000 for a total of $2750, divided by your hourly rate. Instead of 30 massages, you need to do about 43 for the month. But, by having a specific dollar figure in mind and knowing what percentage of your fees are going to business expenses, you can assess how to achieve that objective realistically.

EXAMPLE: *If you want to take home $2000 personal income, every month + you need $750 to cover monthly business expenses = $2750 (before taxes) is the amount required for you to generate in monthly massage business revenue.*
$2750 ÷ $65 hourly rate = 43 massages required in a month to cover expenses, before taxes.

Myth 3:

All my clients will be steady and loyal forever.

It would be nice if you could rely on clients, at their first session, to schedule, in advance, a weekly massage for the next twenty years, but people aren't robots with endless discretionary income. Whether a client gets massage for relaxation or pain management, there will come a time when he/she stops coming to you. There are an infinite number of reasons, few of which have anything to do with the quality of technical service you provide. People change, and their priorities change with them. People lose their jobs and are forced to cut back; some move away. Others, regardless of their satisfaction, simply get massage for special occasions like birthdays or anniversaries.

Less dramatic, life-altering events also play a role in the choices people make about massage. They get sick or go out of town or have any number of unexpected conflicts arise. Even when they schedule a session with great anticipation, clients cancel, leaving empty slots in your appointment book. Basing the success of your practice on a finite number of regular clients is just too risky because at the moment you feel secure and confident in that future revenue, you will lose a couple of them for their own personal reasons.

> *Whether a client gets massage for relaxation or pain management, there will come a time when he/she stops coming to you.*

The trouble massage therapists run into is banking on those "regular" clients, both consciously and unconsciously, at the expense of continually attracting new clients. Most people, including massage therapists, prefer the familiar over the unknown, and it's very easy to get in a rut. Joanne always comes on Tuesday at 2:30; Beth always comes on Wednesday at 10:00; Roger always comes right after Beth. You unintentionally start anticipating those clients' sessions without any guarantees. When a client has shown some degree of consistency, it's natural to assume you are giving them what they want. Since no one would not want massage, it's difficult not to get trapped into thinking that client will just keep coming week after week.

Unfortunately, if you look at your calendar and see it booked with those clients you can "count on," you fail to see other opportunities. If you have fifteen clients who have come to you every week for six months, you may tell yourself you can't handle more clients, or you don't want to do more than fifteen massages a week. But what happens when one client is transferred to another city, another one loses his job, and another one can no longer fit that massage into her schedule or budget? If you've been blinded by the past display of loyalty and regularity, you won't have anyone in reserve to replace that once steady income. If you maintain those "regulars" for a certain length of time, ask yourself how much trouble it really is to do an extra two or three massages periodically. Those infrequent clients do nothing but add to your business. Sometimes they will provide additional income; sometimes they will replace the income you expected to receive from your "regulars." Avoid a disastrous outcome; don't allow yourself to classify your clients as "sure bets" and always be on the lookout for new ones.

Myth 4:

I'm going to give massage to anatomically perfect people.

Most massage therapists, including ourselves when we started, have preconceived ideas about the kinds of people who will come for massage. There is an assumption that certain individuals, for various reasons, aren't comfortable being relatively naked in front of a stranger. It may be due to weight or age or physical deformity, but the fact is people from all walks of life, with all forms of physical eccentricities, will want massage from you.

There aren't going to be many clients who have 2% body fat, unblemished skin, minty breath, pristine feet, and shower-fresh scent. People are overweight, obese in some cases, have scars and sores and pimples, and come for their massages twelve hours after they last brushed their teeth or bathed. Usually they will not resemble magazine cover models or professional athletes. Most clients will be "normal" in the sense that they will have their own unique personal characteristics—some of which you may find offensive or, worse, repulsive.

The academic setting doesn't prepare you for this unsettling experience either. No one can teach you what physical traits bother you or how to move beyond them when they arrive on your table. It is one of those lessons you learn "on-the-job." Often you don't even realize you have an issue until you literally uncover a client to begin the massage. Then, it's too late to decline your services. You've made a commitment, and if you are unable to overcome your personal feelings, your client will feel your discomfort or disgust through your hands.

> *There aren't going to be many clients who have 2% body fat, unblemished skin, minty breath, pristine feet, and shower-fresh scent.*

Not only is this detrimental to getting that client to return, it isn't healthy for you either. Both of us have had experiences where we had to overlook the outward appearance or odor of a client to do our jobs effectively, and it wasn't always easy. Once you fully recognize and appreciate the individuality of your clients' bodies and your personal reactions to them, you won't be overwhelmed when a seemingly unpleasant circumstance arises. It's best to define what physical attributes and idiosyncrasies cause you to feel anxious and work them out on your own because inevitably the kind of eccentricity—hairy backs, cigarette smoke, stinky perfume, missing body parts, rashes, bumps, or pimples—you most dislike will be some of your very first clients.

Myth 5:

I'll get my practice off the ground
by working on friends and family.

While friends and family sound like the most obvious place, right out of school, to find (and keep) clients, it is usually a really bad idea. Your circle of friends and your family are the most difficult people to work on because you have established relationships with them. They know you first as a buddy or a daughter—someone with whom they've eaten meals and celebrated birthdays—not a professional massage therapist. You undoubtedly also carry a certain amount of baggage in relation to friends and family, and making a clear distinction between you as friend and you as a professional service provider will be difficult on both parties.

There is also a built-in component of power in your role as a massage therapist. Friends may genuinely want massage from you but may misunderstand the boundaries and control you're required to maintain while you're in session. The same is true with family members. You must perform the techniques you've learned without having to think about the fact that your mother or brother is lying vulnerable on your table or that during last summer's family reunion the situation got a little heated over the potato salad and a game of horseshoes. It's impossible to divest yourself of all the previous experiences, good and bad, you've had with a family member or friend, and while you shouldn't necessarily refuse massage to people you already know, you need to be very careful.

> *You undoubtedly also carry a certain amount of baggage with relation to friends and family. Making a clear distinction between you as friend and you as a professional service provider is difficult on both parties.*

Your friends and family should be a ready source of support and encouragement as you embark on your new journey as a massage therapist. Recruiting them as your first clients can be seen as an obligation in which they may or may not want to fulfill, and it can lead to bad feelings. You may resent their unwillingness to support your practice financially, and they, in turn, may not be too keen on paying for what they think their friend or family member ought to do for free. You're much better off to attract clients you don't know, so you can establish yourself exclusively along the lines of a professional service provider.

Friends and family can be an unbelievable marketing tool though. Who else knows you better and can sing your praises? We will cover the role they can play in building your business and how you can capitalize on them in a later chapter.

Myth 6:

I'll have all the clients I can handle
through "complimentary" businesses.

New massage therapists mistakenly believe they can procure a steady supply of clients by letting other alternative health care-related businesses know about their new practices. There are really two misconceptions here. The first misguided belief is complimentary businesses like chiropractors, spas, gyms, and health food stores are waiting and anticipating your arrival and marketing material. The second misguided perception is that you are the first and only massage therapist to come up with this idea.

We were guilty of this misguided attempt to woo the alternative health establishment into sending us clients. We wrote letters to every chiropractor in town, believing they would enthusiastically welcome our invitation. Not a single one responded. Beyond the fact that these businesses receive dozens of identical solicitations annually, promoting someone else's business is usually not in their best interests. Massage therapists conceive this idea while still in school because the benefits of massage do often go hand-in-hand with other types of care, and in the course of study, the obvious, though wrong-headed, assumption is those other practitioners need massage therapists to add credibility to their own services.

Massage therapists often see themselves at the bottom of the alternative health hierarchy, and so to establish their own credibility, they need another business to advocate for them. Essentially, what the massage therapist sees as a perfectly symbiotic relationship is merely a parasitic attempt to get referrals without offering anything in return. Imagine what you would do if a new esthetician asked you to send your clients to her simply because she was available. You'd probably be reluctant, if not downright uninterested. Believing any business, complimentary or otherwise, will line their own clients up outside your door simply because you exist as a massage therapist will most likely result in a healthy dose of disappointment.

Massage therapists begin their practices thinking of themselves as well-intended saviors. Their belief and intention is to give pain relief, comfort or pampering to everyone who has muscles to massage. They see the rewards of massage as the only necessary requirement for convincing clients to call, so they wait for those people to arrive, primed and ready for a good experience. When the phone doesn't ring, they began to worry about how they will survive and start looking desperately for some connection to save them. This act of desperation leads many massage therapists on an unsuccessful and time-consuming venture that actually takes them farther from their objective of gaining new clients. Any healthcare or complimentary business interested in offering massage as a corollary service for their clients has probably established relationships with credible, experienced, reliable therapists long before you ever graduated from school. The businesses that do not refer clients to a massage therapist usually aren't going to change their minds because you have now presented them with your cover letter and brochure.

> *Any healthcare or complimentary business interested in offering massage therapy as a corollary service for their clients has probably established relationships with credible, experienced, reliable therapists.*

Putting 100% of your efforts into attracting one field of complimentary professionals or health-related stores is never a good idea because the time and money you invest in securing a single referral source won't give you the return you expect. Massage therapists tell us, "If I could just get a doctor on my table, I'd be set." One individual, whether it's a medical doctor or a chiropractor or a tanning bed owner, can never supply a massage therapist with enough business to sustain a growing practice. If you're looking for a complimentary business to save your struggling practice, you're missing the broader panorama of opportunities available and within your individual grasp. We will talk more about referral business in section 4.

Myth 7:

My clients love my service, so they'll
love me and be my friend too.

Just as new massage therapists believe friends and family or complimentary businesses are the way to jumpstarting a practice, established therapists can get fooled into believing their longstanding clients want to be their friends. Massage clients, especially ones who have been repeat customers, genuinely like massage and appreciate their therapists. It doesn't mean they want to be personal friends. There is a natural intimacy and bond between client and therapist, but it is founded, and should be developed and maintained on clearly defined professional grounds.

Some massage therapists lose sight of this fundamental principle because they confuse the satisfaction a client expresses about a session - with a personal affirmation of themselves. We don't mean you shouldn't be warm and inviting or honestly care about your clients, but you can never forget clients pay you to perform a very specific function for them. While they may compliment you and even refer business to you, they see you as a service provider—just as they view their doctors, hair stylists or personal trainers. Consider your doctors and decide how many of them you plan to be friends with, discuss your personal life with, or visit at holidays.

> *You overstep your boundaries when you assume clients want anything in addition to massage.*

Still, massage therapists feel "connected" or "in tune with" their clients because of the intimate nature of massage, and it is true there is a greater level of proximity. That doesn't mean a client wants to detail her problems with her husband or ask your advice on quitting his job. You overstep your boundaries when you assume clients want friendship and counseling on anything not related to massage. It's like walking up to a stranger and starting a conversation nose-to-nose. However comfortable you may feel with that kind of closeness or however much you may feel you need intimacy for your own personal self-worth, resist the temptation to view clients as potential soul mates or bosom companions. Clients who feel pressured by an inappropriate interest in their private lives will stop scheduling appointments. If you're desperately trying to befriend clients, even if you might not describe it as such, your practice will suffer significantly.

Myth 8:

My practice will grow by word-of-mouth.

It is true word-of-mouth is an extremely powerful method for getting your name out. The problem is you have absolutely no control over what gets out about your name. Have you had a client come to you a couple of times and never schedule a massage again? What are they saying about you? Maybe she was unhappy with what you did and is telling everyone **not** to call you.

People who are happy with an experience take it for granted. When we purchase anything—services or products— we expect them, at least, to meet our expectations. When we're satisfied, we don't usually go to great lengths to tell everyone we know about it. But, when a purchase fails to live up to our expectations, we're ten times more likely to complain to a friend. Take for instance a meal at a restaurant. Once you're seated and select your meal, you assume the server will bring you what you ordered, keep your drinks full, and basically look after your dining experience. When your order is wrong or the server disappears for forty-five minutes, what is the first thing you do the next time someone asks you about that restaurant or where to go out to eat? "Don't go there; the service is horrible." You don't take into consideration the server's bad day or the party of sixteen he got stuck with right after you sat down. You just have a bad taste in your mouth about the whole place.

It's a common human characteristic, and because not every single person who ever gets a massage from you will have a mind-blowing experience, you cannot rely on them to promote you. We've had clients come happily to us regularly for years and never once think about referring another person to us. If someone were to ask them about massage, our name definitely comes up, but relying solely on existing clients to "sell" your practice to others is a risky proposition.

> *Word-of-mouth is only one of a dozen tactics you should actively employ to attract new clients*

New practices often have no one who can pass their names along to others, but consider again Myth #5 regarding friends and family. Massage therapists attempting to convince friends and family to be clients also think they will be walking billboards for them. People, no matter how much they like you, are too wrapped up in their own lives to remember to talk about your business. As far as existing clients go, a weekly or monthly one-hour massage is a relatively small part of their total experience, and though they may anticipate the massage before arriving and bask in the feeling afterward, it doesn't automatically cross their minds to go immediately and directly to their own friends, family, and business associates and tell them to call you as soon as possible. Word-of-mouth is only one of a dozen tactics you should employ to attract new clients.

Myth 9:

If no one is on my table, I'm not working.

New and established massage therapists believe this misconception. As far as business goes, the actual time you spend giving massage constitutes a relatively small part of your day, and an even smaller portion of building a business. Think about it: when someone has scheduled a massage, and is lying on your table, you have secured only one fee. There's no guarantee this client will reschedule or tell anyone else about you. When you begin to believe you're only working when you have a client, you misunderstand the impact of owning your own business.

Let's uses a hypothetical example; if you were employed as a bank teller, would you ever consider leaving the bank because no one was in line to make a transaction? Would you say, "hmmmm, I have no customers, I think I'll go to the grocery store?" It sounds ridiculous when you think about it in terms of working for someone else. Why? Because, your boss would remind you of your obligation to the employment contract. As a self-employed business owner, you are the boss. You have to tell yourself to keep working the business. Distinguishing time with clients as work and time without clients as your own personal time won't get you many new clients.

> *As a self-employed business owner, you are the boss. You have to keep working the business. Distinguishing time with clients as work and time without clients as time off, won't get you many new clients.*

We talk to many frustrated massage therapists who complain about the lack of clients, but they're only in the office if a client is scheduled to be there too. When you conceptualize work as only the time you are giving massage to an individual client, ask yourself what did it take to get that client on your table in the first place. Did she appear out of nowhere? Did he call out of the blue? Wasn't the time and energy you used to sell your services to that person part of the workload? The attraction of clients is just as much a part of your day as performing the massage, yet so many massage therapists view the between massage times as "time off the clock."

We'll cover this issue more in Chapter 4, being unavailable is no way to entice callers or build credibility among other therapists who may be calling to ask if you'll handle their overflow. When you don't answer your phone, don't expect people to keep trying to reach you.

Myth 10:

I tried marketing, and it didn't work for me.

Compare marketing to the action of sleeping. You sleep in order to stay awake and have energy. If you don't sleep, you have no energy. Marketing is also designed to give your business energy. Marketing is designed to place your name in front of potential buyers. Marketing requires time. Marketing requires planning. You market your business to influence the decision-making process. Marketing makes consumers curious to get more information.

To suggest marketing doesn't work is as silly as claiming that sleep is not restorative and money won't buy you things. Marketing works if you're doing the right things. We make suggestions to massage therapists when they question us on what they should be doing. When we propose a strategy for them, many times they say, "I tried that once, and it didn't work." A one-to-one ratio doesn't work in marketing. One marketing objective does not result in one client. There's usually no direct or immediate correlation between a marketing tactic like giving free chair massage at a health fair or offering a discount to the local gymnastics team and acquiring clients. Marketing is about the constant, repetitive, successive exposure of your business to those prospects you are targeting. It is essentially a one-to-one-to-one ratio where each marketing message builds on the previous one to create a lasting connection between you and the buyer. Consumers need repetition to notice and become interested in a product or service, and by consistently putting your name in front of them, the Law of Averages works in your favor. Consider the marketing strategies of McDonalds or Coca Cola. Studies suggest it takes seven separate exposures to a product before a consumer makes a decision to buy. If you try something only once, you severely limit your ability to show prospects what your business can do for them.

> *Studies suggest it takes seven separate exposures to a product or service before a consumer makes a decision to buy that product or service.*

You cannot look at marketing as an event; it is a process. Plus, it isn't something that works for some people and not for others. Many massage therapists throw the baby out with the bath water because they expect a single effort to result in instantaneous client bookings. When that doesn't occur, they strike that particular tactic off their list forever. If you don't get the results you were expecting, first you need to reexamine the situation and decide what caused it to be unsuccessful. Your expectations may have been unrealistic. When you put a flyer up at the local gym, and nobody called to schedule, was it the flyer's fault? Or, was it posted along with fifty other flyers on a bulletin board? Or, was it because you listed all the modalities you are trained to perform but failed to mention the words "massage therapy"? Your meager results have nothing to do with utilizing a flyer; it has everything to do with the manner and frequency in which you tried to use the flyer.

Obviously, some marketing strategies work better in certain circumstances and with different kinds of people. The main thing to remember here is: Marketing does work! Marketing **IS** how you grow your business. Let's rephrase that. **Marketing is how you grow your business**. If you've shuffled all forms of marketing off to the side as a waste of time, what soon won't be working is you.

Conclusion

If you're feeling a little lost about how to proceed, don't worry. While there are a number of myths you should definitely get out of your head, our intentions aren't to leave you with a list of don'ts. We had to learn the hard way—by trial and error—and we made many mistakes along our journey. (We wasted a lot of time and money too.) What we discovered in the process was our understanding of how to grow our business was only slightly off center. We knew no one was going to serve us up a full plate of clients without our direct involvement, but we never let go of our desire to be massage therapists. So, hold onto your dream and implement a few good marketing strategies, and you can grow your practice according to your goals. It doesn't matter if you're a **Career Changer**, and this venture has to work or else. It doesn't matter if you are a **Discretionary Income-Maker,** and you want to create a little more stability within your practice, and it doesn't matter if you are a **Young Graduate** who never wants to work for someone else. It can work, and you can make it happen.

The misconceptions so many massage therapists fall prey to are really no one's fault. Owning a massage therapy practice isn't easy, and growing one doesn't come by way of magical incantations or ethereal dreams. The challenge you face is identical to every other small business owner in the world: attracting and retaining clients. The remaining chapters in this book are marketing **principles** on which you can base your marketing **decisions**.

The progression of chapters is to start with principles to attract new clients then how to retain existing clients. Finally, we offer principles for creating a productive, sustainable referral base. None of these three areas are mutually exclusive because hopefully, you will be involved with people who fit each category. So, depending on where you are in the development of your practice, you can freely move in and out of each section without missing anything from preceding chapters. And, because we aren't giving tips, you have much more flexibility in using the principles in your own creative ways. By trying to explain the overarching ideas in each of these critical components of a successful, thriving operation, we're forcing you to do your own "brain" work for concluding how they might be utilized within the context of your personally defined ideal practice. Though it may be tougher than being spoon-fed a series of actions to take, you will develop a much greater ownership of how you employ the tactics based on the principles. And ultimately that will take you down the path of achieving your personal and professional goals.

Chapter 3

Summary and Things to Consider

10 Myth Summary

Myth 1   Because I am a massage therapist, clients will automatically call.

Disarm Myth 1. Arm yourself with statistical information. Check out the websites for National Certification Board of Therapeutic Massage and Bodywork, American Massage Therapy Association, Massage Therapy Foundation and the Associated Bodywork Massage Professionals, and others that you can find. Most have the latest industry information and fact sheets obtained from research and consumer surveys.

Myth 2   I'm going to make $60-70 per hour.

Disarm Myth 2. When planning your budget, remember that expenses and taxes will have to be paid first. And even when working at full capacity, figure that you can probably only do 25-30 hours of massage work every week, so base your budget on this number.

Myth 3   All my clients will be steady and loyal forever.

Disarm Myth 3. Even regular clients change their minds or have schedule changes. The majority of the general population don't receive massage on a regular basis. Realize that you will have far more clients that receive massage once a year than those that receive massage once a week.

Myth 4   I'm going to give massage to anatomically perfect people.

Disarm Myth 4. Imagine every conceivable possibility and how you will react to that situation.

Myth 5   I'll get my practice off the ground by working on friends and family.

Disarm Myth 5. Build your own business relationships. You'll be glad you did.

Myth 6   I'll have all the clients I can handle through "complementary" businesses.

Disarm Myth 6. Build your own business relationships and you'll get referrals from those relationships.

Myth 7   My clients love my service, so they'll love me and be my friend, too.

Disarm Myth 7. Remember your professional boundaries. Define them before starting your practice - not on an individual basis.

Myth 8   My practice will grow by word-of-mouth.

Disarm Myth 8. Word of Mouth and Referral Business are 2 different animals.

Myth 9   If no one is on my table, I'm not working.

Disarm Myth 9. It's a job. Put in 40+ hours a week building your own business, just like you did working for someone else and you'll be successful.

Myth 10   I tried marketing, and it didn't work for me.

Disarm Myth 10. I wonder where McDonalds would be today if they didn't continue to market their business.

Section II

Attracting Clients

Attracting Clients

How many of your new clients do you already know? Since you have no established relationship with most new clients, it is imperative to attract them. Marketing doesn't work like a faucet you turn on and off depending on your need for water. There's no machine across town ensuring your pipes are full and ready to provide you a steady stream of business. Marketing is a perpetual state of mind; it is multi-faceted and varied because the relationships you have with your clients are in innumerably different levels of closeness. You may have developed a strong association with your "regular" clients, and some of them may even send you referrals, but there are others who have only received a single massage. There are the vast majority who have never experienced your table and most likely don't even know your name. You have to market to each kind of client (or potential client) differently.

Attracting clients is, by far, the most complex piece of the marketing puzzle. Acquiring new business through specific marketing strategies is also what so many massage therapists give up on or attempt with inappropriate and unsuccessful tactics, even though it is the most important facet to building a thriving practice. If you have only a vague notion about who is out there to become a client, then your marketing efforts are bound to be hampered by misconception and missed opportunity. There's great confusion between attraction and retention, and many marketing gimmicks massage therapists employ to gain new clients backfire because the marketing message assumes a relationship that does not yet exist. For instance, we saw a print advertisement several years ago with a headline that read, "Feel the Love" for a Valentine's Day promotion. It may sound cute and appeal to you, but marketing isn't about what you believe is catchy or fun or even important, and being in the massage therapy profession, "feeling the love" isn't really the professional message we want to convey to the general public. It is all about effectively communicating with the person on the receiving end of the message. When you presume a level of intimacy with potential clients, like associating yourself (as a stranger) and your service with the traditionally personal holiday, there can be a subconscious, and sometimes conscious, negative reaction to the message and, by extension, you.

If your practice is brand new, attracting clients may be the one thing you think about all the time. "How can I make the phone ring?" If your practice has become a little stagnant or you've lost a client or two, you may be deciding what direction to go now. Regardless of your length of time in business, you cannot retain clients you don't have. Spending your marketing budget on methods that assume familiarity or suggesting your name is sufficient reason for patronage will result in huge disappointments.

> *Regardless of the length of time you've been in business, you cannot retain clients you don't have yet.*

Marketing offers no magic bullets for success. Take some time to reflect on the following principles as ways to reevaluate your mindset when it comes to business growth. They don't represent a list of specific exercises or step-by-step guidelines. These principles are more about attitude—your own strategic attitude about how marketing can significantly impact your business's bottom line. And they will. In the end, how you promote your business initially to relative strangers determines the rate at which your practice will grow. Think like the client. Know your audience. Gain their perspective. Once people become clients, then you can address how to keep them (Section 3) and how you can develop sustainable referral sources through business relationships (Section 4.) Until then, you must concentrate on developing your own mindset about where to find those potential clients and how you can most effectively reach them and persuade them to try you.

Chapter 4

Principle 1:

Live Your Business

*"Sadly, many people are either afraid or unwilling to fully
immerse themselves
in the possibilities that surround them at work - or, for that
matter, in life.
They do what is expected, and that is all."*

~ Joseph A. Michelli, The Starbucks Experience

The day you opened the doors of your practice you became an elite member of a relatively small group of individuals called CEOs. In the business community, there are two kinds of people: owners and employees. Owners make decisions, offer direction, create the vision, and lead; employees carry out that mission by following the rules. There is no difference between the role you play in your massage therapy practice and the CEO of a large corporation. Big companies may have hundreds of staff members who do specific tasks, boards of directors who offer guidance, and shareholders who hold the organization accountable, but ultimately, the company succeeds or fails based on how the leader conceptualizes the organization and reaches the goals. While you probably wear every hat—from accountant to purchasing manager to marketing director to therapist—it is still your primary responsibility to ensure the business is successful.

Who are the single most recognizable people in the computer software and afternoon talk show industries? Bill Gates and Oprah Winfrey are household names today because they represent their respective companies with an unwavering dedication to promoting their products. They market. They advertise. They strategize. They live their business. You are no different as the sole proprietor of your massage therapy practice. While your name may never reach global proportions, consider who you think of when a casual conversation turns to a local tanning salon, spa or coffeehouse? Isn't there an image and a name you associate with the most prominent and successful businesses in your area? Every owner of a business started out with nothing more than a product or set of skills, a location for operating, and a goal, and that's exactly what you have as a massage therapist. You have a license to practice massage and, hopefully by now, an office to conduct those services. However you've conceived your business, you also have a goal for success.

It is how well you promote yourself that makes the difference because every other massage therapist has the same basic skills and a place to work. As an employee, work is simply a necessity you participate in each day in order to maintain your current lifestyle. Owning your own business isn't the same thing. As a business owner, there are no time sheets, performance reviews, or people to cover for you when you don't feel like working. You **are** the business, not a cog in the machine. You are the face representing your business of massage therapy to the public. In a way, you can never be an anonymous individual again, but that doesn't mean you don't receive substantial reward for doing so.

> *We see ourselves as business owners 100% of the time—with a client, at a hockey game, on vacation, or at home. We are business owners. Our business happens to be massage therapy.*

Because your success or failure depends solely on you, understanding the principle of "live your business" is critical to developing a successful practice. Live your business doesn't mean "working all the time." Massage therapists who know us often claim we're successful because we're "always working," but they confuse the number of hours we work with our devotion to maximizing every opportunity. Because our business and massage practice is predicated on who we are, we don't have competing roles in our lives. Our personal lives and our public occupations wrap around each other, and though we may spend more time "working" than some massage therapists, it is because we don't characterize ourselves as business owners and massage therapists only when we're with a massage client. We see ourselves as business owners 100% of the time—with a client, at a hockey game, on vacation, or at home. We are the business. We are business owners. Our business happens to be massage therapy. If we don't capitalize on every opportunity, another massage therapist will. Living your business means more about staying constantly focused on who you are and striving to achieve your goals. If you see yourself as a business owner, whether you have a client on your table or not, you become more aware of the availability of prospective business.

Your marketing efforts reinforce this idea in the minds of those you are trying to attract. They don't think of you as a massage therapist for an hour once a month; they associate massage therapy with you, so to them, you are massage therapy in its entirety. Clients aren't steeped in massage therapy the way you are, but when they think about a massage, whether it's at 4 AM or 11 PM, your business should be exclusively on their minds. When you live your business, you effectively project to everyone you encounter what you do and who you are—no matter what the circumstances. It has nothing at all to do with when you are in your office. If you see yourself as a massage therapist only when you have a client, you reduce the chances of building your practice substantially. You have to realize whenever someone is having a conversation with you—on the phone, at a dinner party, or in your office—she is speaking with a licensed massage therapist, a business owner. So, you must respond accordingly.

It doesn't mean you are slaving away at balancing your checkbook at midnight and ignoring your family. It doesn't mean you have to adhere to an impossibly inflexible regimen. It simply means you no longer transform yourself into a worker from 9 to 5 with a specific job description. You're allowed and encouraged to integrate your personal life into your business. As we said in the opening chapter, doing so is quite liberating because you don't have to define yourself by opposing role requirements. It gives you the ability to see the broader picture of who you are in and out of the office. It's no longer a burden because the person you are in private is no longer distinguishable from the person you are in public. Your business is based on you, so if you naturally are light-hearted and fun-loving, then you don't have to create a reserved, cautious persona when you're dealing with business tasks, with clients or without them. The mantra of corporate America tells you to leave your individuality at the door, but when you own your business and live your business, you get to honor who you are all the time. And because you make no shift in how you define yourself when the whistle blows, you're more attentive to the possibilities of attracting new customers, new clients.

> *The mantra of corporate America tells you to leave your individuality at the door, but when you own your business and live your business, you get to honor who you are all the time.*

Living your business isn't just about how you represent yourself and how others see you. It's about always being present in the world that includes your profession as well as your individuality. When you're a business owner 100% of the time and an opportunity comes up, you don't say "When I get into the office, I'm going to have to get in a business mindset and do something about that prospect." Take that moment when the potential client is prepared to discuss her massage needs to initiate the beginning of the relationship. If you tell a caller you will call them back when you get in the office, you're almost always going to lose your chance. People are impatient and fickle. If you can't handle their needs when they want them handled, most of the time they will keep searching. When you receive a call at home, be aware that to the person who has called, you are still a business owner, even if you're cooking dinner or watching TV or playing games with your children.

When you live your business, an unexpected call means potential. If you receive it when you are technically "out of the office," you have to realize your business isn't bound by the walls of your building or the time slots in your appointment book. If you continue to make distinctions between who you are "at work" and "at home," you hurt yourself by not being authentic, and that attitude comes across to your clients because you are merely putting on the mask of a massage therapist during the sessions.

Many massage therapists misunderstand being constantly on the look-out for business opportunities means giving up everything else in life, including the freedom and flexibility they've become accustomed to. We all have non-work-related tasks we must accomplish, but the time spent buying groceries or attending PTA meeting doesn't mean you've stopped being a business owner. If it is impossible to speak at length with someone inquiring about your business, take a brief moment to establish a foundation for yourself, so when you can return the call, you'll have something to build on. Taking the time, even if it is only for two minutes, to be fully engaged in a phone or face-to-face conversation, the potential client will feel like you've respected her initiation of a possible relationship and will be more willing to wait several hours or until the next morning to discuss her situation with you in more depth. If you spend those two minutes explaining how you aren't at work or can't talk (or you don't even answer the phone at all,) what motivation does the prospect have to pursue any additional conversation with you? Plus, if you tell yourself you're "not working" when you're attending to personal activities, you won't see the person staring at you from across the cash register or your child's teachers as potential clients.

This difference between always working and always being aware of what you're working for is important. For us, it is very casual to be at home engaged in a family activity and for one of us to have a thought about the business, make a comment, and go right back to what we were doing. It's not that we brought our work home with us. There wasn't a deliberate plan to spend all day giving massage to clients and come home to a stack of paperwork to complete while ignoring the family. Because we are both massage therapists and we both own the business, we are each other's natural sounding-board, so it is easier to have business-related discussions interwoven into the general home-life conversations.

Our situation is relatively uncommon. For most of you, you are probably the only massage therapist in the family or the only business owner in the family, but you have to be comfortable having a business thought or idea in the middle of a family event without feeling like you are diminishing or ignoring the immediacy of the present circumstance. You aren't shifting your attention between two opposing areas of importance because your life is no longer compartmentalized like that. Recognizing an opportunity or making a connection to your business success in the midst of a family- or personally-oriented activity isn't the same as the corporate manager hunched over a laptop furiously completing a project for a deadline while any engagement with the personal side of life is put on hold. As a business owner, you have continuity in your situation the corporate worker doesn't have. They see two choices: they can finish their work at the expense of their private lives, or they can jeopardize their careers by actively participating in their families. As a business owner you don't have to live that kind of dual existence where someone always ends up losing.

Living your business becomes a very positive exercise because not only does it require you to recognize and honor consciously who you are all the time, you function in a state of total integration. It allows you to appreciate a late phone call at home as a possible long-term client rather than an interference. You aren't interrupted because no matter what you were doing before the call and what you will do after the call, you never stopped being a massage therapist/business owner. Work isn't consuming when you define it this way because you always function within the scope of who you are.

> Living your business becomes a very positive exercise because not only does it require you to recognize and honor consciously who you are all the time, you function in a state of total integration.

Many massage therapists tell us their efforts to attract clients often fail to meet their expectations. They are usually looking for a qualitative result, i.e. ten letters sent out should equate to at least two new clients, or a free chair massage event should reap several on-the-spot bookings. Marketing isn't about direct results most of the time; the one-to-one ratio of cause and effect rarely produce an immediate transaction. There is a process of introduction, rapport, and trust. When you live your business, you stop calculating your success by the number of clients who responded or didn't respond to an offer or incentive. Remember that research suggests it takes 7 times, 7 hits, 7 different levels of recognition before the consumer reacts and makes a purchase. By constantly being attentive to opportunities, you market your business in a steadier, continuous method (the one-to-one-to-one ratio.) It is this accumulation of efforts that spur prospects to act. Most of the time you will never know exactly which one of your marketing strategies tipped the scales and caused someone to call.

Struggling massage therapists have grudgingly told us they were going to have to get a part-time job to support them until their practices got more stable. Although taking a part-time job will help cover immediate expenses and commitments, it limits your ability to remain focused on the full-time requirements of your business. Instead of seeing the business as failing, work it. Not having a client doesn't mean you aren't a massage therapist or a business owner. It simply means you have the opportunity in your day to expand your business by putting yourself and your name in front of people who have never been on your table. If you've ever had a job before, think about how you worked. During your scheduled

40 hour workweek, you hopefully completed your tasks, got promoted for exceptional work, etc. You have to put the same kind of energy into your massage therapy practice as you would a job as an employee for someone else. This may sound a bit remedial, but we see massage therapists all the time who complain they aren't getting enough clients but spend an entire 8 hour workday totally detached from their business simply because they didn't have a client scheduled. You reap the greatest rewards by the things you do when you **don't** have a client on your table.

Practical Application: 1 – Schedule Your Work Week

One of the easiest, most effective ways to put yourself in a position to succeed is to think of yourself as an employee. By this, we mean designate a schedule for your self. If you're intent on building your practice, we suggest developing a 40-hour work week. If you see yourself as a **Discretionary Income-Maker**, forty hours may be more than you're willing to invest, but make a certain hourly commitment each week in which you are focused on your business. If your practice is your sole source of income, it is crucial to devote a substantial amount of time each day to business development. Most people define a job as working from a starting point and continuing to an ending point. They associate "work" as taking place during those hours. When you choose a work schedule, whether it's

9 to 6 Tuesday through Saturday or every morning from 8 to 12, you choose to be actively engaged in all aspects of your business.

If you're renting your space on a monthly basis, you have a perfect environment to concentrate on marketing and building your practice when you don't have clients. Say for instance, you have only two clients on a given day, one at 10 AM and one at 1:30 PM. If you arrive at 9 to prepare for your first client, as soon as she leaves, conceptualize the next couple of hours as uninterrupted time to brainstorm and research possible avenues. When your second client leaves, instead of shutting down for an early afternoon of running errands or cleaning the house, focus your attention on how you can attract more clients; create a flyer, make phone calls, scan the newspaper. If you work from a flex space where you rent it specifically to conduct your services by the hour, find a quiet place somewhere else to concentrate on marketing. It can be the library, the local coffeehouse, or your basement, but discipline yourself, in the beginning, to spend those hours you aren't giving massage to clients to explore your business opportunities, brainstorm ideas, and formulate a plan.

It isn't necessarily glamorous, but consistently spending time each day on activities to build your business is like investing money in the stock market. You don't expect the stock market to deliver a return or dividend the following morning. You invest it for the future, and when you visualize your non-massage efforts as investments, you move away from the quantitative mentality of this-for-that. When you set up a time clock in your mind for when you will be at work, you begin to see ways to connect to the community, to specific groups, to previously insignificant events. It is this active process that makes the difference. You aren't going to get new clients by sitting and twiddling your thumbs any more than you are by giving a one-hour massage and then going home until the next appointment.

The bottom line is this: if you aren't focused on attracting new clients, no one will do it for you. By being in your office or "on the clock" for a predetermined amount of time each day, you make yourself available in ways you don't if you're at home or driving around town running errands. Whatever marketing you may have done, people who are searching for a therapist generally call a number of therapists before deciding which one to use. When you aren't there to answer the phone, the potential client crosses your name off the list and goes to the next one. It's the first person the client talks to and feels comfortable with who typically gets the booking. Most people new to massage don't shop around like they might for the best bargain on new shoes; they decide based on their instincts about the phone conversation. So, after you've done some marketing—a letter in the mail, a free event, a promotion— answer the phone. As few calls as come in, someone needs to be there to take them when they come. You will never know when someone may become interested in your services. Something you did six months before may result in a call.

When we started our business, we committed ourselves to office hours, even though there weren't any clients to begin with. We arrived at our office at 9 AM every day and developed a practice of studying our marketplace. As we mentioned before, we did some things we thought would be profitable, like mailing a letter to every chiropractor in town, expecting referrals to come like manna from heaven. But we also did other things that did eventually pay off because we didn't give up on them, even when it didn't seem like they were generating any business.

Sitting alone in your office contemplating how you are going to make your practice grow can be daunting. When your table is vacant, consider exploring these options.

- Research your local newspaper's weekly calendar of events and plan to attend some events with business cards in hand,
- Scour the Internet for information about your community and utilize the information to create a marketing strategy,
- Use the newspaper to discover groups and organizations making headlines and then contact them with proposals, offers, or discounts,
- Send letters or postcards to the people you've recently met, offering a discount to come to the office,

- Introduce yourself to your business neighbors and ask them to post your information,
- Visit networking groups and develop strategic business relationships,
- Study business trade magazines for other people's successful marketing ideas,
- Attend business shows and seminars (many are free to the public) and take business cards and brochures,
- Explore the benefits and costs of joining your local Chamber of Commerce,
- Read everything you can about massage techniques and begin to specialize.

Doing some of these activities every day open up vast areas you may have never considered. Selling yourself isn't fake or corporate or compromising your values. It is sound business practice. Go find your clients. Be the opportunity. While many of you may see these things as pushy or forward, if you don't do them, another massage therapist will. And, that person will be your community's Oprah Winfrey of massage therapy while you're wondering if you made the right decision to go into this field in the first place.

Practical Application 2—The Introductory Speech

Massage therapists make people feel good, right? Is that what you tell people who ask what you do for a living? Telling someone you "make people feel good" can have a hundred different connotations, some of which, as a massage therapist, you don't want to convey. When someone asks you what you do, do you have a rehearsed script with which to respond to that question? You should. When you live your business, you should be prepared to explain what you do in a very personal and convincing manner at any time or place. But know your audience. If you're talking to a young mother, you probably wouldn't talk about the muscle soreness associated with sitting at a computer. Likewise, you wouldn't explain the benefits of sports massage to an 80-year-old grandmother. But, if you don't know how to explain yourself beyond "I make people feel good," you will miss excellent opportunities to develop relationships with new people.

An introductory speech is a short, concentrated explanation of what you do. It isn't the technical aspects of your services either. It is a simple way to fuel a conversation. It's an opportunity to connect to another person. When someone asks you what you do, say you're a professional massage therapist, and immediately find out what kind of person he is by asking him questions. Does he work in an office all day in front of a computer? Is she a soccer mom? When you have acquired some information about the other person, you can better explain on a personalized level what you do in terms he or she can appreciate and understand. Consider the office worker scenario. A woman tells you she's an administrative assistant and asked what you do. You could say you make people feel good, or you could say, "You know when you're sitting at the computer, and it's four in the afternoon, and you start to feel your shoulders ache and burn?" When she says yes, tell her, "I stop that pain through massage we can relax your shoulders." You've given a very specific explanation of how you make people feel good, but it is one that is immediately recognizable as a benefit to that individual. Anyone who has ever felt that sensation at the end of the day will appreciate the description and the possible solution from you.

Having a series of introductory speeches is critical. You can develop a very general speech to recall when you don't know anything about a person, but you should have a number of variations you can automatically pull out of your arsenal to explain what you do. When you can express your occupation from several different perspectives, you won't get tongue-tied when you speak to people. Consider all the different kinds of people:

- office workers, professional athletes, or students
- stay-at-home moms, someone recovering from a car accident, or runners
- school teachers, retail sales people, traveling sales people
- CEOs, surgeons or pregnant women.

Creating these introductory speeches is something tangible you can work on during your "office hours." It is important you know how your speeches sound. They shouldn't sound robotic or canned. Can you sing the song by heart or do you have to use the sheet music? Practice them out loud until they sound natural and automatic. Listen to the message they convey because the objective is to reach that person directly on how massage can benefit them specifically. It's also the best way to keep a conversation going. But remember, it doesn't mean the person is going to call you the next day to schedule a massage. It simply means you have positioned yourself as a knowledgeable professional, a solutions-provider, and you've planted the seed in that person's mind about your business.

That seed will only grow if you feed it, and when you see your marketing efforts as a garden of sprouts, you will be more motivated to build on what you've started. So, by creating a schedule and a plan for you to work on every day, regardless of your appointments, and by developing several variations of the description of what you do, opportunities won't pass you by. In fact, you will begin to see them in more and more places. You'll see chances to get your business in front of potential clients. The results will fuel your desire to continue the process. You'll be able to say without hesitation, "This is who I am. This is my business"

Chapter 4

Summary and Things to Consider

Principle 1: Live Your Business

- Be available.
- Answer your phone.
- Keep office hours.
- Define your schedule - ahead of time.
- Be ready to react.
- Take last minute appointments.
- Define your Introductory Speech, your elevator speech, the critical 30 second "Let me tell you who I am and why you should come to me for massage" speech.
- Define your answering machine message.
- Define ahead of time, the answers to the questions you know you'll be asked.

Chapter 5

Principle 2:

Find a Group and Be the Expert

*"Start wherever you stand,
work with whatever tools you may have at your command,
and better tools will be found as you go along."*

~ Napoleon Hill

Theoretically, you can offer your services to any person with a set of muscles; furthermore, you can provide massage indefinitely because there will always be a population with muscles to massage. But, "Anyone" can be surprisingly difficult to find. "Anyone" has no address or phone number. "Anyone" has no schedule or specific need. "Anyone" doesn't even have an understanding of why she needs massage. Conceptualizing your target as "Anyone who has sore muscles," or "Anyone who wants to be massage" often leads to finding "Nobody" instead. "Nobody" comes to massage therapy practices every day, and unfortunately, "Nobody" has cash to pay you. "Nobody" can't tell others about how great you are, but for many massage therapists, "Nobody" is their most loyal repeat client.

Massage therapists, and small business owners, stumble and get confused about how to define who will most benefit from their services. Because you know and fully understand everything about massage therapy, it is easy to look at the broad picture and tell yourself they all could use massage and wonder why they aren't responding in droves to your marketing. While "Anybody" can indeed benefit from massage, there are five problems with why it is ineffective to market yourself broadly as a method for attracting a steady flow of new clients.

Problem #1—The general populace doesn't understand the need. Collectively speaking, they don't realize what massage can do for them personally. They hear the message, they understand the message but they can't relate to the message. When you attempt to reach a large, unrelated group like "Anybody"in your community, there is not enough commonality among them for your message to be understood personally en masse.

Problem #2—The general populace isn't searching for that need to be met. Because they don't relate massage to their need, they aren't actively looking for the solution. There is no association in their minds between the pain or discomfort they might have and the benefit of massage to relieve those symptoms. Most advertising or marketing campaigns they encounter typically come from larger companies like spa and resorts and suggests to them expensive, unnecessary or irrelevant to their circumstances. They associate the random encounter with a massage advertisement, as they would junk mail or spam. Any consideration is tossed away and forgotten almost instantaneously.

Problem #3—The general populace can't discern your marketing from the rest. People are bombarded with mass generalized messages enticing and encouraging them to make a purchase. These messages usually have nothing in common, so it isn't a matter of simply competing with other massage therapists. You're also competing with the car dealerships, shampoo commercials, insurance, holiday sales at the mall, coupon mailers, and all the other advertisers attempting to reach thousands of prospective clients without knowing whether or not there is any need. Your message, even with a discount, will often be lost in the mix. Make your follow up marketing material relevant to the group you are targeting in order to get their attention. Whatever you send out should remind them specifically of you and how they met you. If you are targeting pregnant women, don't send information about deep tissue massage. If you're targeting runners, don't send pre-natal material. Make your message stand out by addressing the immediate and specific need of the intended audience.

Problem#4—The general populace doesn't think about massage consciously. It isn't constantly on their minds, which is why people don't call you the minute you open your doors and activate your cell phone. The fact that you're in business means little or nothing to their daily lives. They are schoolteachers and construction workers and convenience store clerks. They are mothers and fathers and church members and soccer coaches. They are engaged in the immediate dynamics of their lives just as you are. Massage and specifically you as massage; just doesn't register on their radar screens like it does for you.

Problem #5—The general populace doesn't view you as a useful resource. Presenting yourself as a valuable, trustworthy service provider is more about how you see yourself, not necessarily how strangers might view you. To them, you're an unknown quantity, even if they have some interest in massage. They may receive a letter from you or see your flyer posted on a bulletin board, but that alone isn't enough to sway them. Marketing and advertising to a faceless crowd assumes a relationship you haven't yet established, so with nothing but your word to go on and no immediate need, typically, people don't take any action.

Most massage therapists wouldn't characterize their attempts to attract new clients in this manner, but many are, in effect, trying to sell their services to "Anyone" and getting "Nobody." If someone asked you who you work on, does your answer begin with "Anyone who…?" If you characterize your clients and prospective clients in this nondescript manner, you can expect to remain an anonymous entity for the majority of them. Your marketing efforts need to be specialized and concentrated to be effective. "I work on people just like you, who…" It doesn't mean you're excluding certain types of people or missing out on business. It's quite the opposite. Define and market to a specific variety of groups. Create boundaries for yourself to keep you focused. This is the real key. You must identify who constitutes the groups you're interested in pursuing—and then you have to be relentless in that pursuit.

Once you've chosen a group or two, zero in on their commonalities, and be careful because it does matter how you delineate one group from the unassociated masses. Affluent women may, at first glance, seem like a profitable group to invest your marketing into because of their increased spending capacities, but what else do they have in common. Not much usually. The same thing goes for an entire occupation like doctors. They obviously have a similar job, but that doesn't mean they have all the same interests. It's easier to see large groups, based on a single defining characteristic like wealth or occupation, than it is to see the value in a more tightly classified group. For instance, you can market in mass to parents with school-age children, or you can market to the specific parents involved in your child's PTA. You can market in mass to blood donors, or you can work closely with your local chapter of the Red Cross. People gather because of mutual interests and similar goals, so how do you identify groups for whom you can become the sole massage therapy resource?

Two Ways to Define Target Groups

One way to begin this process is to think about 2 things: 1) who do you already have professional relationships with and 2) with what groups/activities do you engage in other areas of your life? In other words, what are your secondary passions? Where do you spend you free time? What subject areas do you know a great deal about? Are you a fitness fanatic? Are you a Sunday school teacher? Do you live in a specific neighborhood, development, or suburb? Are you heavily involved in your children's extracurricular activities? Your secondary passions give you direct routes into established groups because you're not an outsider. You are familiar with what makes the members of the group tick, who better to directly express how massage can help them. For instance, if you happen to be a runner, you know what it feels like to have sore, aching calves. In talking to other runners, you are also simply a person who understands the uncomfortable feeling that can result from a strenuous run. Once in the conversation, you can explain your role as a massage therapist and how you understand how massage can help alleviate that pain. By examining the various groups to which you belong, and share a common experience, you can focus your attention on a relatively small number of people who you already understand from a practical standpoint.

Here's another analogy, if you have nothing in common with a group of young parents, how would you connect to them in any way other than as a person selling services? You'd quickly be reduced to spouting out generalized marketing information. On the other hand, if you are a parent you remember what it feels like to have a baby hiked up on one hip while you're trying to cook dinner. You understand the resulting back pain because you experienced it personally. You also have a great deal more to talk about than just massage therapy because you can relate to all the aspects of parenthood. When you can communicate to a group, "specifically", you are less of a threatening salesperson and more of a person they would most likely chose to do business with given your commonalties and professionalism. You're involved in a conversation, you've began to establish some professional relationships and can establish the necessary level of trust that allows you to put some heart into relaying your specific, focused marketing strategies and extends an invitation for them to come visit your office. This method of connection is a genuine approach to present your authentic self, even though your primary objective is to become that group's massage therapist. You're meeting new people every day through your own interests and connections, how easy it is to invest where you're already personally vested.

The other way to target and choose specific groups is to consider with whom do you already share professional relationships? Can you utilize the relationship with your former employer to offer free chair massage to all the administrative assistants? Does your hair stylist complain about stiffness at the end of the day? Is your child's baseball coach also the director of human resources for a local company? Do you know the chairperson of a local non-profit organization where you already donate some of your time? When you think about all the people you know, consider the fact that they are all members of groups. Those groups could be professionally related to occupations or through interest groups and charities, but rather than spend all your time approaching total strangers, invest your time in planning how you can capitalize on relationships you have already developed. Acquaintances and associates will always be more willing to listen to you than someone with whom you have no prior relationship.

Utilizing a friend or colleague to gain access to a group you are not personally a member of lends credibility to your presence. Other members will be more attentive and responsive when they know you are there at the request of one of their own. You will still have to develop your own relationships as an extension of your introduction into the group, but you will be able to do so with greater speed and a higher likelihood of success. Say, for instance, you aren't an athlete but want to target people who participate in outdoor sports. Do your research about who you know and what they do, then learn about that particular activity. Once you've done that, approach your neighbor or dentist, or whoever it who is an avid hiker and a member of the backpacking club. Sell him on your idea and then let him advocate for you to the members. He will have more influence over his group decision than you would if you approached the same group directly. Because each of you knows a completely different set of people, take a moment and think about who you know and the groups to which you're connected. Make a list of possible target groups you'd like to be involved with. Develop some creative ways to position yourself, through these people you know, as that group's massage therapist. Once you have won that group, decide if it works for you, what about it works, and how you can make it better. Then, expand your view outward from that group. Who are the people on my list and what other groups are they involved in and connected to? Now, begin to build on what you've already created.

Be Massage Therapy

The groups you target need to think of you when they think of massage. Be massage. You need to be the single individual that comes to mind every time massage is part of a conversation. The only way for that to happen is to stay consistently in front of them. Once you have outlined which groups you plan to target, repetition will be the most important element for solidifying yourself as the massage expert to them. When you constantly cause the same set of people to recognize who you are and what you do, eventually, they will think of you exclusively as massage therapy, even if you haven't yet convinced them to schedule an appointment. To them, you **are** massage therapy. Be massage. Be massage therapy, to them.

For instance, if you decide to target cyclists, you should attend every weekend event they have and volunteer your professional services to give free massage at the end of the race. When you establish yourself as a fixture at the weekend events, the members will see you shopping at the grocery store or sit next to you at a restaurant sometime during the week and make the connection. "Oh, you're the massage therapist that comes to our races." It's that "Ah ha" moment that you're looking for. You want them to associate your name with massage therapy. You're that massage therapist. When that moment of recognition occurs, and it will, you reinforce in their minds who you are and what you do. It's not ever about only getting that one individual cyclist to come in; it's about getting that individual cyclist to recognize you as massage therapy, and begin to generally refer to you, and about you, in conversation with other colleagues. Those several hours you spent rubbing out cramps for free each weekend though can transform you from a novelty to well known expert that other cyclists turn to for all their massage needs. You get strong name recognition from the group members and, by extension, regular paying clients.

Because the members of the cycling club associate you with massage therapy, your future marketing messages come through more strongly. If you've been to every race for two months and you send a letter to each person you've given free chair massage to during that time, you have a much better chance of having it opened. They will see your name and recognize it. Likewise, when they have conversations with non-cyclists, your name will immediately come up when the discussion involves massage. "We have this massage therapist, who..." By targeting the cyclists, you may get clients seemingly out of the blue because the group for whom you are the expert is talking positively about you to people you don't even know.

If, on the other hand, you decide to target cyclists and go to only one event to offer free massage, no one will remember you in a month. When you pursue specific groups, you have to give yourself some time to become their expert. It won't happen automatically after one exposure to them. If you say, "I tried that, and it didn't work," you're making a huge mistake. It wasn't that you chose the wrong group or they weren't interested or you did something that "didn't work." Each event builds on the other and the each time you present yourself to the groups you've chosen, you put yourself one step closer to that moment when they make the connection themselves, instead of you doing it for them.

Repetition, Repetition, Repetition

No matter how much you may want it to be true, people aren't going to react with triumphant joy the moment you enter their lives. They simply are not or were not waiting for you to enter their life, and your initial split-second presence into their day is not enough to make a marketing difference. Consider how you, yourself, are convinced to spend your own money. Let's say a massage table manufacturer got your name from a list of recent graduates and sent you a letter saying, "Hey, we know you just graduated from massage school. We know you need a massage table. We sell them. Give us a call." If that brand was unknown, and you never heard from that company again, what would compel you to buy from that company? You'd probably buy your table from a company you kept seeing in magazines or heard about from others. It may have been a perfectly good table to use. The successful company knows even the most targeted consumers have a very specific reaction to memory when it comes to making a purchasing decision.

The same principle applies to marketing efforts applied to groups. A one-shot attempt to convince a group to listen to you about your massage business just cannot be heard over the volumes of advertising messages. Let's say you targeted the local gardening association because they bend and squat and would be good candidates for massage. Think about all the gardening information, magazines, products and services those specific gardeners are bombarded with in the course of a month. Whether they are reading, shopping, handling product, or reviewing their junk mail. You're competing with hundreds of other companies for attention. You're marketing along with companies that sell tulip bulbs, pruning tools, chemicals and magazine subscriptions. Your one letter or flyer or chance encounter is too easily lost in the volume of information and advertisements they receive. If you are a gardener yourself or your best friend knows the president of the rose association you have a greater chance of being introduced, complimented and referred.

Getting into a group may start with a free event like offering to speak at a monthly meeting about the benefits of massage. Couple that speaking engagement with a drawing for a free massage. The drawing entries give you a <u>free</u> mailing list. Because you are already more knowledgeable about massage than any member of the group, you can find a creative angle to present your service to them in a way they will immediately understand. The gardeners may have never thought about the fact that massage could lessen the pain they feel after planting their spring flowers or weeding their vegetable gardens. They will recognize the connections though when you explain why they hurt and how it can be reduced or avoided. Then, you have to keep your name in their minds. Send a letter or offer an incentive for a massage directed at low back pain relief for club members. Your repeated efforts will pay off in the long run because you will be the sole massage therapist they think of every time they stand up and stretch their backs. It may take several months before anything happens, but if you have consistently put your name in front of them as a resource, the first time they're aching and sore they'll think, "You know, I should give that massage therapist a call."

A Personal Example

A local company called us to provide free chair massage at a health fair. We attended the health fair and followed up with letters of appreciation. Several months later the company had an international conference with twelve VIPs coming in from out of town and wanted us to provide massage for them. One health fair and several targeted reminders of who we were, resulted in those twelve massages. Instead of randomly searching for a massage therapist to do the work, they called us because we were **their** massage therapists. We transformed a free health fair for the company's employees, costing several hours of our time, into the beginning of a business alliance that may lead to more work in the future. If we had gone to the health fair yet never made any further contact with that company or its employees, we would have missed the bigger picture. We would not have become the face of massage therapy for the entire company's needs.

Repetitiveness gives the impression of success, consistency and longevity. Have you ever wondered why the major soft drink and beer companies still put ads on television? Surely everyone in the world knows those products are available to buy, but through the repetition, they project an image of a successful company because how else would we all know about them if they weren't doing something right? This same principle can happen to you. Assuming you are marketing to the right people, every chance you get to make a strong connection between yourself and massage therapy promotes your image as a successful business owner. Just because someone doesn't drop everything and come running to your door doesn't mean your tactics aren't working. Again, consider your own purchasing decisions. Remember the law of 7, repeat your message 7 times and 7 different ways. How many one-time advertisers do you remember buying anything from? You possibly received a coupon, but then you saw a billboard or a company vehicle or even the company logo on someone's shirt. Then you read an article about them, and then you found that coupon again – which reminded them of you again. Without any conscious thought you started to believe that this company, of which you have a coupon, must be pretty good. You think you're seeing them everywhere. If you do a free chair massage event for a group, you're strengthening that group's impression of how successful you are.

Let's go back to the cyclist example. They see you every weekend at their races, but they aren't just cyclists – what else do they do? They are also members of many other kinds of groups. They may work at a local corporation where you've agreed to participate in a health fair. They also may be involved in the Chamber of Commerce where you're doing free chair massage for a monthly after hour's event. When the people in your chosen groups begin to see you in places other than group functions and activities, they will assume you must be fairly successful. When people start saying, "I see you everywhere," you're on the right track. Those people's assumptions will become your reality, and one success leads to another because individuals want to do business with companies they believe are successful. When prospects believe you are "everywhere," the cumulative effect fortifies your position as the exclusive massage therapist in their minds. Even if you haven't been in practice for very long, if you continually represent yourself as the expert to specific groups, they will believe, through your consistency and repetition, you have a useful service for them.

> *When prospects believe you are "everywhere," the cumulative effect fortifies your position as their "go-to" massage therapist.*

Our practice is successful because we kept going after the same groups over and over, even when it didn't seem like we were bringing in any new clients. The letters we sent or the free massage we gave away were never considered "events," in the sense of being singular functions. Each marketing message accumulated in the group's collective mind, and eventually, they had that "Ah ha" moment. It is a long-range mentality. Many unexpected outcomes happened as a result of investing ourselves in specific groups and becoming their experts. But, it was never overnight. Being patient when the bills are due is no easy task, but if you look at the time and money you spend marketing to a targeted group and become their exclusive massage therapist, you will begin to see positive, often unanticipated, results.

The Group Beyond the Group

There's a common tendency when marketing to specific groups to overlook additional opportunities because you're so focused on one set of people. Whenever you target a niche, you must remain cognizant of the possibilities associated with that whole group. For example, we targeted participants in a local fundraising race. The organizers brought in massage therapists to offer massage to the participants of the event. We could have easily centered all of our attention on the people in the race, hoping to capitalize on their athletic pursuits as an indicator for their future needs for massage. But we didn't stop there. In addition to the individuals in the race, we wanted to be known as massage therapists to everyone at the race. So, instead of concentrating exclusively on the actual runners, we also wanted the sponsors, vendors, and event staff to recognize we were the massage therapists associated with the race.

By broadening our scope and looking for the next circle outside the immediate circle, we were able to see direct opportunities for relationships with a much larger group than just the race participants. We established ourselves as the massage therapists to everyone at the event and leveraged that common bond to make solid connections to everyone associated with it. At that point we could say to sponsors and vendors, well after the function was over, "We were the massage therapists at race," and they would say, "Oh yeah, I knew I recognized you." We had been attached to the same set of circumstances, so we were not strangers to them. This gave us the potential for all future marketing efforts and business opportunities to have a greater impact on them directly. We were able to follow up with them as we did with the actual runners, but with a slightly different slant—one that would be relevant to their unique circumstances.

Another example of the "group beyond the group" is our experience with the local ballet company. We negotiated some advertising on trade. We received an ad in the show programs in exchange for providing the professional dancers with free weekly massage. It didn't matter if the dancers chose to come for their massages, and at first they didn't. We were getting free advertising for nothing. But we wanted the dancers to come so we created a flyer to post at rehearsal to remind the dancers about the free massage. To our naïve marketing mind what happened next as a result of that flyer was completely unexpected.

A student dancer saw the flyer, and she convinced her mother she had to go to the same massage therapist as the professional dancers. The mother scheduled an appointment for herself, and shortly after, the daughter was coming too. Then the other daughter came, and then the grandmother came, so on and so on. We had been targeting people attending the ballet with our advertisement, but we reached an unplanned group as a by-product. The students and their parents became part of that group who saw us as massage therapy. The mother and daughter became regular clients, even when our original deal with the ballet company was completed. They had made the connection that we were massage therapy. We could have been satisfied to get the ad in the program without any out-of-pocket expense, but we knew if we were going to become this group's massage therapist, we had to do more than wait for people to respond to the ad. By branching out and putting our names in front of everyone associated with the ballet company, we increased the power of the original deal.

We have countless examples of how we've attracted new clients who were not our primary target within a group. You never know who your prospects truly are. You may be trying to attract participants at a fundraising event only to discover one of them is also the purchasing agent for corporate gifts. The groups you target will most likely have offshoots you can take advantage of. They are like spokes on a wheel. There is the center, your primary group, but there are spokes in every direction leading away from the one group to another. When you are looking for additional opportunities within a group, they will present themselves more readily. Once you have begun the process of becoming the massage therapist for a group, start examining the circumstances to see what else might be available. More times than not, you will find correlations you couldn't have imagined beforehand. As you make your name known in one circle, those relationships and contacts lead to other opportunities, as well as strengthening your brand awareness in the community. Eventually, by becoming various groups' massage therapist of choice, your name will overlap between groups, and someone from the gardening club will also see you at her son's cycling race and then see you at her company's health fair. On and on it goes. Once you become "the massage therapist" for one person, you also become "the massage therapist" to everyone that person knows. As long as you narrowly focus your view in the beginning about what defines a group, your repeated efforts to "Be massage therapy" will reap significant rewards.

> *Once you become "the massage therapist" for one person, you unknowingly become "the massage therapist" to everyone that person knows.*

Chapter 5

Summary and Things to Consider

Principle 2: - Find a Group and Be the Expert

- Start by defining your target market:
    o Define personal interest groups
    o Define who you already know
- Be Massage Therapy to that group.
- Repetition - hit that same group over and over again.
- Once you've exhausted that group - look at the secondary groups behind that initial group.

Chapter 6

Principle 3:

Always Do Pro Bono Work

"To affect the quality of the day, that is the highest of arts."

~ Thoreau

Pro bono work is often misinterpreted as giving away your services for free. Unfortunately, this mentality is the exact opposite of the truth. While you may receive no real dollars when you agree to participate in an unpaid event like a health fair or special corporate function, absolutely nothing you do related to marketing your business should be considered "free." Everything comes with a price—and usually a reward—yet many massage therapists balk at the thought of providing their services at no charge. Everything you've been taught in school has prepared you to be a genuine, fee-charging massage therapist. You have your certification; you passed your state licensing exam. You are a legitimate member of the business community, and businesses charge money for their products and services. That's what business is about, right? Fees for services? I do this for you, and in return you pay me hard currency.

Generally speaking, yes, you are in business to earn a living, and you can't do that unless people pay you when you give them a massage. The need to be financially secure often takes precedent over everything else, so some massage therapists believe doing massage at no cost after graduation is equal to business suicide. Many people view their practices this way. They simply refuse to engage in any event when someone calls to ask if they will do free chair massage. This is not business suicide. Business suicide occurs when no one knows you. Business suicide occurs when no one knows you have a business or what the business offers or where you are located. Offering your services at no charge is advertising. Offering your service at no charge is a long-term principle like everything else in this book. It isn't a tactic designed to bring in immediate clients; it is about exposure. There is no simpler way to get in front of potential clients than participating in opportunities where money doesn't change hands. When it comes to marketing your business, money and time are interchangeable. You can save one by spending more of the other.

> *When it comes to marketing your business; money and time are interchangeable. You can save one by spending more of the other.*

First of all, your business is a tactile one. You touch people. What better way to make a connection directly with them. But in order to touch them you need to be in the same location. A bundle of brochures and a stack of business cards placed indiscriminately on someone's counter, where you believe the clientele would be interested in massage, gives you absolutely no chance of physically being in their presence. A health fair puts you in direct contact with attendees. If you work a health fair for five hours, you have the potential to <u>show</u> 25-30 people, in real time, how massage can benefit them. There will be those individuals who simply want the free fifteen minutes of massage and nothing else because they already have a therapist, but there will also be people who don't associate massage therapy with anyone. Those people are ideal candidates for your future marketing. They are like blank slates, looking for people to fill all the slots and all you have to do is write your name in the slot for massage therapy. The only way those people will associate you with massage therapy is if you have a chance to touch them and make a connection.

The second reason "free" events are such promising opportunities is there's no buying pressure. The participants don't have to have their guards up about being sold to. They can enjoy the brief encounter with you in pure enjoyment, so when they think about you, the **only** thing they think about is how perfectly pleasant the experience was. There isn't a better way to begin a relationship than when people have nothing but praise for you. They don't have to weigh the satisfaction of the chair massage against your assertiveness in trying to schedule them to come to your office. They don't have to do anything because you aren't forcing them to make a decision. You want them to stand up and say, "That was fantastic. It was just what I needed." If you follow the compliment with, "When would you like to come in for a full massage?" you have interjected an unnecessary irritant. It's like screaming into a bullhorn, "Okay, get ready for my sales pitch!!" Not exactly the most intelligent thing to do to someone you met fifteen minutes ago.

Develop a Marketing Budget

Like most marketing strategies, engaging in pro bono work, doesn't usually result in immediate, tangible monetary outcomes. That doesn't mean it isn't vitally important to include as part of your overall marketing plan. While you most often don't pay cash to do free events, like you would for an advertisement in a newspaper or magazine, there is still a cost attached to your time. Very early in our practice, we set up a time-based marketing budget (appendix A), and in doing so, we assigned a dollar value to everything we did related to building our business. We determined we had to invest $1500-2000 per month, (23-30 massages) in marketing if we were going to grow. Obviously, we didn't have that kind of cash sitting in our bank account to "spend" on advertising, but all marketing isn't about expensive ads, slick brochures, or fancy websites. In fact, when you don't have a lot of money, your time is the most valuable asset you can utilize to get your name in front of potential clients.

You have to shift your mindset about marketing from expense to investment, especially when it comes to choosing to participate in non-paid events. So as part of our marketing budget, we designated free chair massage to "cost" $65 per hour per massage therapist. If we did an event for ten hours with one massage therapist, we "spent" $650 of that $2000 for the month. If two therapists worked that event, we considered the total marketing investment to be $1300. Every letter we mailed to prospective clients, as a result of those events, cost 50 cents (paper, postage, and time.) Any networking function we attended received a dollar figure based on how long we were there, 2 hr event × $60/hr = $120, "spent" on that function. Absolutely everything we associated with marketing our practice counted in the budget, and we knew if we "spent" $2000 every month, our practice would grow. We also knew many of our "investments" wouldn't necessarily bring us a quick return, but would pay off in the long run. It's like putting money into a retirement account. You don't view those funds as "spent" income. You don't expect to wake up the next morning and be independently wealthy, but over time your discipline provides you a financially secure future.

Whatever your current financial situation may be, it is imperative to rethink how you value unpaid massage. We're not suggesting you won't be successful without having a $2000 marketing budget, though you'd be surprised how quickly you can reach that amount by consciously assigning dollar figures to all your activities. The size of your budget is based on your goals, but you do yourself a disservice to say you can't afford marketing because of the expense. If you're just starting your practice or you're currently working part-time but wanting to add to your client base, begin with a smaller dollar amount and increase your budgeted amount over the next several months. Just keep in mind you also get to allocate a dollar figure for the time you spend putting together a deal, the time you spend in your office researching groups, and the time you spend actually giving massage pro bono.

As a business owner, how many advertisements have you bought because an account manager convinced you his publication's demographics would be well-suited for you? And then gotten no calls? Here's a tip: the people who sell ad space have only one objective in mind when it comes to talking to you, and it really has nothing whatsoever to do with growing your business. They are working. This is their job. It is their job to sell the space in exchange for a paycheck. The same mentality applies to people attempting to sell trade show booths. They are trying to fill the spaces, not grow your business. We've known massage therapists to rent booths at trade shows and spend $300-$3000 actual dollars but in the same breath turn down a human resource director's invitation to come out for a company's health fair for no charge. The same types of people attend both events. Why would you consider the tradeshow legitimate marketing but the health fair exploitation? If you see all the events you participate in as investments, which is better on a day you have no clients: paying $400 to stand in a booth for eight hours hoping attendees will remember your name and call for an appointment or to stand in a booth for eight hours giving chair massage to fifty people, at no expense to you, and receiving their names and addresses to add to your mailing list.

As far as trade shows go, they are good exposure, however; you are better off to offer to do free chair massage at someone else's booth. The traffic they will receive because they are offering you as an incentive to come into their booth will be tremendous. You keep people hanging around and standing in line. Approaching companies already planning to be at a trade show and suggesting you give free chair massage to anyone who comes to the booth won't be treated lightly. Every trade show booth participant is looking for a gimmick to get more people to stop and look. They are looking for "the draw". Why else would they give away pens and stress balls and free prizes? When you can be a company's giveaway, a company's booth draw, you will probably be remembered long after the event. Find out when the next trade show is in your area will be and call several companies attending and ask them if they'd like to offer free massage in their booth. More likely than not, they'll be stumbling over themselves to get you first and may even offer to pay you all or a partial amount of your time.

It's hard to keep from getting frustrated when all your money seems to be going out rather than coming in, but when part of your marketing budget is composed of events you don't have to pay for with cash, it is much easier to stick with it. If you're spending several hours giving free massage, consider the alternatives. You could be spending hundreds of dollars on an ineffective advertising campaign and getting no clients. You could be doing nothing but waiting by the phone and getting no clients. Isn't it better to be in front of potential clients where you have direct control of the situation, even if no one becomes a paying customer the following week. You will have a stronger impact in person rather than hoping someone sees your ad or brochure at the exact moment in time it's available. When you do a free event and give your time a monetary value, it will be a positive experience, and you'll be able to say, "I touched thirty people today, and I had no out-of-pocket expense." Viewed from this perspective, it's a whole lot easier to look at the next month and believe the next free event you're asked to do will be worthwhile.

The 70/30 Rule

Not every unpaid event is a good idea. Just because a location is available to offer free chair massage doesn't mean you're wisely investing your time to attract recognition and clients. Many massage therapists are oblivious to the 70/30 Rule. Seventy percent (70%) of the population has never gotten a massage and don't associate massage therapy with any particular therapist. They are unaware. The remaining thirty percent (30%) of the population have an awareness of massage and had massage in the past and may even have a regular therapist. Many massage therapists attempting to attract new clients are investing their time in trying to convince the 30% of "aware" clients to come to them while ignoring the larger "unaware" population. For instance, agreeing to provide free massage at the grand opening of a health food store may sound like the most ideal place to gain exposure, but not if you weigh the facts. The massage therapist believes the patrons of a store like this will be open to massage and more ready to schedule appointments, so she targets that opportunity. The problem is these people **are** definitely perfect candidates for massage, because they already get massage and already have an established picture of who represents massage therapy to them—*their* massage therapist. It's not going to be altered in a fifteen-minute session with you, but they will thoroughly enjoy it and will definitely take advantage of the offer. More times than not they'll leave the store thinking, "That was nice I think I'll give *my* massage therapist a call."

You did nothing wrong in your technique, and you will likely be able to touch a lot of people at a health food store because they don't have to be convinced to receive it. They are thinking, "Hey, free massage! Cool. Let's go." At first, you'll think you made a wise decision, but your opinion will change when they all start naming their therapist or reveal they are a therapist themselves. Massage therapists are notorious, if not incredibly receptive and open to volunteering for free chair massage. Instead of trying to convert those individuals who already get massage or know the value of it, look for places where the 70%, who don't already get massage, will be. You may have fewer interested passers-by, but the ones you do touch will be primed for your marketing after the event. Would you rather give free massage to twenty people who have a massage therapist or ten people who have just experienced massage for the first time?

Where are these places? All around you. A little creative thinking will get you a long way. Consider your neighborhood grocery store or businesses that sell sporting goods or clothing. There are literally hundreds of businesses where you live you can target. Just realize there are many more places where the people are not already massage enthusiasts. Businesses with an ideological connection to massage, like a health food store or a New Age boutique, may be initially easier to convince, but they also have had a dozen other massage therapists trying to do the same thing. So not only are you futilely going after the already-taken crowd, you're competing with other therapists all fighting for a few crumbs.

Once you have an ideal location to offer free massage, don't plan on filling up your calendar the same day. In fact, LEAVE YOUR CALENDAR AT HOME! Keep in mind the people you will come in contact with aren't going to be ready for a verbal sales pitch, and they probably won't want your business card either. Instead of having a mindset of needing to schedule them, because you're desperate to get paying clients, simply have them complete your intake form and let them go. Once the event is over is really the time you can begin to entice these potential clients to come see you. Send them a letter thanking them for the opportunity to work on them and offer a discount off their first visit to the office. First of all, they will recognize your name because the experience is still fresh in their minds, and, secondly, a letter is non-threatening and gives them a chance to respond on their own terms. Many of them might not act, but that doesn't mean your name isn't still the one they associate with massage. That letter or business card magnet might stay on the refrigerator for three months, but when they are ready, they're going to call the one person who represents massage therapy for them...meanwhile, every day they see your business name.

When you decide to do an unpaid event, you always need to answer the question, "Why am I doing this?" Too often massage therapists view their marketing activities apart from themselves. If you are approached to offer free massage, does it fit with who you are and what your practice represents? Is this one of your target groups? Are the attendees more or less likely to be familiar with massage? Is the event associated with someone to whom you already have a connection and add value to you attending? What are the ramifications of spending your time in this manner? If you can't answer all these questions, step back and objectively weigh the pros and cons. Saying yes to anyone and everyone who wants you to provide free massage is just as potentially harmful for your business as flatly telling everyone no. You have to ask yourself, "Is this a group I want to be associated with or not?" By utilizing the 70/30 Rule, you can make this decision in a more intelligent way. Is the group more likely to be in the 30% camp or the 70% camp? Will I be marketing to the 70% who have never received massage, and ultimately build my business over time?

As we mentioned in the last chapter, repetition is extremely important to success. When you decide to do a free health fair, plan on signing up for the next scheduled health fair before you leave. If you wait to see if anything comes of your participation, you'll be missing the point of doing it in the first place. Remember: Every opportunity you have to put your name in front of the same type of people is your investment in the future of your business, even if you're participating in an annual event. The more often people walk up to you and say, "Hey, you're that massage therapist," you'll realize you are making an impression. All those touches add up to opportunities.

Gift Certificates as "Free" Advertising

Massage therapy is a fantastic gift to give someone else, and you, no doubt, offer gift certificates to people to purchase for that purpose. Selling them is an excellent way to boost your sales and positive cash flow during the holidays and any other special occasion, but have you ever been requested to donate a gift certificate to a fundraiser? Charity organizers are usually scrambling for every business they can get their hands on to give products and services to auction in order to raise money for their particular cause. They are not always discriminating in what they ask for and they typically sound as if they are begging for a handout.

Many massage therapists look at this <u>opportunity</u> as exactly that—a handout. They feel taken advantage of. They see themselves forfeiting a paid massage, so someone else can collect the money. But, let's examine it a little closer. Assume you give a gift certificate for a 1 hour massage to a silent auction. Scores of people will walk by those tables and see your business name, for which you paid nothing to have happen. The people attending the fundraiser have a vested interest in being there to support the charity, but they also want to "win" the items on which they are bidding. Competition can get pretty heated at some of these events, and while your gift certificate might not be the most prestigious prize to be won for the night, the people who bid on it want to win it. They **want** that massage, so they're motivated, interested, and willing to give their money to charity to get it. When they redeem it, what do you have? You have a person who is proud of her prize, excited about the actual massage, and grateful to you for having given her the chance to win it. But, she really paid for it, and if she paid for it once, she'll pay for it again—directly to you. You're actually the bigger winner because what you donated to charity has won you a potential regular client.

This person is someone you may have never had any other chance to interact with, much less get her into your office. But, there she is—ready and enthusiastic. You didn't have to attend a networking event, make a phone call, send a letter, or even knock on a single door to get her to come to you. Someone called you and asked if you wanted to grow your business. They probably didn't phrase it like that, but in essence, that's what they did. They provided you with a hassle-free chance to expand your client base. So, reconsider donating the next time they call.

In the next chapter, we'll be talking about the principle "Never Say No," but here is the one exception to this rule. When a charity calls and asks if you'll donate a gift certificate for an auction, say, "Yes, I'll give you five." Reduce the possibility of that charity calling 4 more massage therapists for the same donation. Think of this opportunity as five new clients. If you only give one gift certificate, then only one person out of that whole crowd in attendance can experience what you do firsthand. When there are five massages to bid on, you know five new people will be coming to see you. It's the only time waiting for clients to walk through your doors actually happens.

Those winners might never respond to any other advertising or marketing you do, but from a simple "Yes," you have real, physical contact with potential long-term clients. In addition to seeing new people for almost no investment of your time, you have a greater probability of retaining one of them for future paid massages. Giving only one gift certificate limits your success rate. That single winner might not be attracted to you, or she might already have another therapist. Many things could prevent her from returning as a regular client, so give your self better odds by giving five instead of one.

The organizers will also be grateful because they are used to being told no. Many businesses—some of them probably massage therapists—view donations as ineffective. By giving more than asked for, you will be remembered. Who do you think that organization will associate with massage therapy from here on out? Who will they call when they need a massage or want to give a gift certificate? Who will they mention when someone asks them about a good massage therapist? The "free" massage you gave to a charity quickly turns into free advertising when people are spreading your name around in a positive light. In the end, it doesn't really matter how someone got to your table. If you can get them there from the minimal investment of a donated gift certificate, you're still promoting your name to members of the community who have the potential to create even more spectacular opportunities for you down the road.

From Pro Bono to the Paralympics

If we had been told the year we started the business that we would be a part of the International Massage Team going to the 2004 Paralympics Games in Athens, Greece, we would have laughed. It was impossible to think anything we were doing at the time would garner such a prestigious opportunity, but in fact, it did. We had joined a local association of businesses, similar to the Chamber of Commerce, so we could network and be a part of the business community. We were offered a chance to provide free chair massage at an Expo for another association member's booth. That event provided the opportunity to build new relationships with individuals involved with the local professional arena football and professional hockey teams. The next year we became the team massage therapists for the athletes.

Through a series of further "free" events and the relationships we developed along the way, we were invited to volunteer in the 2004 Olympics or Paralympics in Athens, Greece. Volunteering meant paying our own way to spend the two-three weeks working on some of the most amazing athletes from around the world. In a sense, it was another unpaid event, but the rewards we reaped from the experience have been far-reaching. When we returned, opportunities became available for media exposure and advertising we could never have afforded before. We did get new clients as well, but more importantly, we reaffirmed our own devotion to massage. We also made a huge impression on our existing client base, which made them even more attracted to us because of what we had given and accomplished. We still don't know what will come as a result of accepting and pursuing this venture. It has definitely opened new doors we had never considered before. And, it all had its roots in a relatively small investment of our time to provide free chair massage for a company who asked.

So, needless to say, we're big proponents of pro bono work. Granted, not every free massage event we've ever done has resulted in such a monumental occasion for us, but that's the thing. We don't know what path will unfold when we give free massage. Even though we have a thriving practice now, we still do pro bono work because it remains to be in the best interest of our community and remains to be the best public relations we can do. There's more to pro bono than being involved in free events like health fairs or grand openings. We also give away massage to individuals who are in circumstances where they can't afford to pay. We're conscientious about when we do this, but when someone's situation is genuinely in dire straits, we know helping that person out will come back around. We may not know the time or the place or the circumstances, but it is in those moments, when we give freely of ourselves and time, that we reap unfathomable personal and professional rewards.

Many times there are opportunities directly in front of us that we fail to see because we're too busy seeing clients and covering our expenses. It is important to have the paying clients, of course, but don't become so tunnel-visioned that you miss unbelievable occasions for future growth. The fact is, some of your current clients will one day not come back to see you for one reason or another, but always being aware of the potential around you gives you an infinite source of possibilities for growing your practice year after year. We are absolutely convinced that pro bono work is a legitimate business strategy for increasing your client base.

Chapter 6

Summary and Things to Consider

Principle 3: Always do Pro Bono Work

- Develop a Market Budget and use it all up in time, not expense.
    - o Utilizing the hourly rate you charge for massage, let's say $65.00, and multiply that by the number of hours you do free massage. Eight hours of massage would subtract $520 dollars from your marketing budget.
- Remember the 70/30 rule: 70 percent of the population have not received massage, 30 percent of the population have a massage therapist...use your time wisely and go after the 70%.
- Use gift certificates as free advertising.
    - o Utilizing the hourly rate you charge for massage, let's say $65.00, deduct that amount for the number of gift certificates you give away. Three gift certificates given to a non-profit to be used in a raffle would be $195 subtracted from your marketing budget.

- Let free chair massage be free. Don't let a tip close the transaction. Let the gift of the free chair massage start the transaction with the hope of a fully paid massage to close the transaction.

Chapter 7

Principle 4:

Never Say No

> *"I am the Master of my Fate,*
> *I am the Captain of my Soul."*
>
> ~W.C. Henley

Like every other business, your job is to help people get what they need. That doesn't simply mean you give them "your dance." Creating a thriving massage therapy practice only happens when you can <u>always</u> satisfy the needs of the people who call you one way or another. The best way you can do this is by never saying no to requests. This principle is critical for establishing yourself as a reliable and dependable source for solutions, even if it might mean you have to work harder in the beginning. Some massage therapists underestimate the impact saying no has on their practices. It seems like a relatively isolated response to tell a caller you cannot see them at a given time because of a conflict you have with another massage or personal appointment, but there are no such things as isolated events when it comes to building your business. Every phone call you get, every event in which you participate, and every chance you have to talk about massage therapy all work together to provide you with opportunities for growing your business.

Still, there are massage therapists who see an inquiry about massage as having absolutely nothing to do with their long-range position as a full-time practitioner. Saying no can cause negative outcomes you may not even be aware of in the moment—primarily, that person will likely never call you again. Likewise, offering to figure out a way to give people what they need, can lead to extremely gratifying circumstances in the future. Several years ago we were in the process of moving from one home to another when we got a phone call. The man wanted three massage therapists that afternoon. Although it was a holiday weekend, and we were not in the office, we asked what he needed. He told us he had promised his soccer team if they made it to the finals of a tournament, he would bring in massage therapists as a reward. Unbeknownst to us, the man happened to be an orthopedic surgeon in town, who was given our name as a referral and who was personally willing to pay for the massage therapists to come.

We couldn't do the work that afternoon because of our move, but we immediately offered an alternative, an option, a solution to his need. We offered to work on the team the next morning at 7 a.m. before their next round of competition. He decided our alternative option would be the better solution. We got all the information, and arrived the next day to do what he wanted. As a result, the surgeon himself became a client of ours, and later, when we applied for the International Massage Team for the 2004 Olympics, he wrote us a personal letter of recommendation which enhanced our eligibility to be selected. We could have done any number of things when that initial phone call came. We could have said, "No, we're in the middle of moving." We could have just not answered the phone since we weren't in the office, or we could have given him the name of another massage therapist, but we didn't. We knew then, as we do now, we only have one chance to accommodate a caller's request, and if we say no, the opportunity is lost. We had no idea taking care of this surgeon' phone call would lead to the subsequent things it did, and neither will you when people call you seemingly out of the blue and want you to solve their problems.

Always saying yes to callers doesn't mean you have to give up your life or control of your business. It isn't about agreeing to do every request yourself. It also doesn't mean we accept the parameters of every request, but we're quick to offer suggestions, solutions and options. You can still do the things you need to do. You can still spend time with your family. You can still maintain control of your business. Saying yes is a marketing tool to add credibility to your practice. When the word gets around that you will never say no, potential clients will be more inclined to call you first, rather than other therapists who have said no in the past. Also, other massage therapists will recognize you as a person to be counted on. When they say no themselves, they will recommend you. Spas and private-practice massage therapists in our area recommend us all the time. They say no but then recommend people call us because they know we will say yes.

> *We've gotten so used to mediocrity and disappointment by service providers we forget how nice it is to do business with someone who will go to whatever length necessary to provide the solution.*

When you can take care of someone's needs, your reputation grows. When you go out of your way to create a viable solution, you stand out. We've gotten so used to mediocrity and disappointment by service providers we forget how nice it is to do business with someone who will go to whatever length necessary to provide the solution. If you build your reputation on quality service and this principle of never saying no, your name will spread like wildfire. It isn't always easy. The concept of putting the client first, can be a hard concept to comprehend or consistently choose. It's not for everyone. When we started our business, putting the client first and agreeing to accommodate a last minute caller meant we had to do the work. If someone wanted a massage at 9 PM, we did it, even if we had been in the office since 9 AM that morning. We couldn't afford not to accept the opportunity because we couldn't afford to let business slip through our fingers even if we weren't completely thrilled with the prospect of working late. But, by first setting the standard ourselves, and then building a network around us, we now have the ability to bring in other massage therapists, who value our client centered concepts, to also do it with us and for us.

> *You have to view yourself as bigger than the hour.*

It may be difficult to imagine though how you can never say no. You are only one person. You have other responsibilities besides your business, and you can only do so much, but the key is, you have to see yourself as *bigger than an hour*. You may be the only person in your company, but your practice is not about individual hour massages. In addition to providing the actual service, you are running a business, and that means seeing beyond the specific time periods of work. When there is absolutely no way you can personally do the work someone has requested, if you figure out the solution instead of declining, your practice will be better off in the long run. There will <u>always</u> be someone who is hungry for the work, and with massage schools graduating new massage therapists every month, you should be able to find someone who will jump at the chance to earn the money. If you don't, your potential client will.

Build your Network - Find Other
Reputable Massage Therapists

Whether you've just recently graduated or have been in practice for a while, get to know other massage therapists in your area. When you have a list of other therapists you can call on at the last minute, you increase your ability to provide for the caller. It also gives you an immediate alternative to telling someone you can't work on them. You never want to take yourself out of the picture. If it is impossible for you to do the massage yourself, coordinating it with another massage therapist still allows you to be the business middleman. If you tell a caller you'll find someone who can handle the request, another massage therapist might do the actual work, but the caller will still view you as the business they turn to for massage.

Why would you send business to another therapist? We're asked that question frequently. Massage therapists complain they don't want to refer the client out or give somebody else the work because they claim it doesn't make sense to help build someone else's practice. They would rather say no and leave the potential client without a solution. When you handle people's needs, either by doing it yourself or sending them to another therapist, you're showing more people the value of massage therapy, you're increasing awareness about massage therapy in general. The more the public understands and appreciates massage the more business there will be for everyone. It isn't necessary to compete with each other and deny other therapists the opportunities because there will come a time when those therapists can't take care of someone too, and will hopefully call you.

When you trust several other therapists, you grow your business simply by having more available time to offer. When you say, "I can't work on you at the time you've asked for, but I can find someone who can," you expand yourself beyond your single pair of hands. When you have a regular client who you cannot see due to a scheduling conflict, asking another therapist to work on him gives you the ability to serve two clients at the same time. Another example of extending your ability to handle business is to subcontract one of the therapists on your list to come to your office and do the massage on behalf of your company. You get the caller's needs met; you provide work to another therapist, and you can make a little money off the transaction. Everybody wins, plus you retain that client because even though you didn't do the work personally, the client still came to **your** office and views **you** as the massage therapist. Situations will occur though where you will not be able to accommodate a caller, and you give that person to another therapist. You're effectively handing that client away altogether, but in doing so, even if that person becomes part of the other therapist's client base, you will have built a stronger bond with the therapist. When they need help taking care of their own clients or potential clients, hopefully, they'll return the favor. Essentially you're helping cover each other's schedules.

Having a group of colleagues within the massage therapy field you can rely on to help you out not only gives you more confidence in meeting client's needs it also gives you the backbone of a network to grow your practice. The more massage therapists you know and can call on to satisfy the needs of people calling the faster your business will grow. When a corporate client calls and needs multiple therapists for a full day, saying no won't even cross your mind because you can coordinate the request. You will have options other massage therapists don't have or don't utilize. We now have approximately 20-30 massage therapists we can contact, at any given moment, even at a moment's notice, to assist us in meeting the needs of our clients. Some are more available than others. Some are more willing than others, but it's a network that extends beyond our two pairs of hands.

Sometimes it is necessary to think outside the box . An out-of-state, human resources manager, from a nationally know corporation, called a therapist in town and wanted 25 massage therapists for 8 hours. The massage therapist told the HR person she couldn't do it, but she gave our company name and number to the caller. The HR person called us, and we said yes, even though there was no possible way the two of us, by ourselves with four hands, could have met that request. We got on the phone and started down our list of massage therapists we knew to see if they wanted to participate. One of the first people we called was the original therapist who initially took the call. We capitalized on a situation the other therapist could have easily done herself because she knew all the same people we did. The difference was we were willing to come up with a solution by using all the resources we had access to—including other local therapists.

Maybe you've never gotten a call like that for a large job, but you will if you're marketing your business properly. When that day comes, you will have your system in place and can say yes without sounding like you're fumbling around. You can simply say, "Yes, I can do that for you. Let me make a few phone calls and call you back." The person on the other end of the line will be relieved and impressed when you can do what he's asked. It won't matter if the need is a single massage you're unable to do or an all-day multiple-therapist corporate event. No matter how large or small the need may be, handling it will only more solidly emblazon your name on his mind when it comes to massage therapy.

How to Satisfy Clients' Needs Every Time

There should be a policy or procedure you use anytime you get a call. It should be instinctive, automatic. Our policy is:

"Yes." Yes to the client's request, so long as it is within reason, within our scope of practice and is legal…we'll figure out the details. As your client base grows and you get more steady business, there will be more conflicts with your time. You will no longer have your entire day available like you did when you opened your practice. It was easy to say yes then because you had no clients. There were no conflicts, but gradually this will change, and the challenge will become more about how to meet the needs of callers. When "Yes" becomes more difficult, you have to know what you're going to say in response to an inquiry. A caller may want a time when you have another client. If saying no is not an option, what will you say? How will you react?

You have to believe you can handle any need, but you must be prepared for your response. When you assume you will be saying yes to everyone, it isn't always necessary to fulfill that request at exactly the time someone wants it. "Yes, however and no, but" will become your first steps in providing a solution. When someone calls for a massage at 1:00 on Friday and you already have that time scheduled, you have to be ready with an immediate answer. "No, but I have 2:30 available." The same is true for an off-site massage in the evening. If the caller wants you to be at his location at 7 PM and that's when you're cleaning up the dinner dishes, you can respond with, "Yes, I'll be glad to work with you this evening, however I have another appointment. I could be there no later than 8:15."

Many massage therapists hear a specific time, look at their appointment books, and say they can't do it at that time and don't offer a solution. That is the end of the conversation. The caller goes elsewhere to find that solution. Being able to offer an alternative time sets the caller at ease because you have made it clear you are willing to help him. People aren't nearly as rigid as they might seem. Just because someone asks for a specific time doesn't mean they aren't going to accept an appointment an hour later or the same time another day. Utilizing the phrase: "Yes, I can, however; or No, but" keeps the conversation alive, and usually that's exactly what the caller is looking for. They want to feel comfortable that the process of securing an appointment will be simple and painless. When you have a pre-determined idea of how to react to a schedule conflict, you sound more professional and thus more credible, especially to people who aren't your clients already. Existing clients will also appreciate you taking control of the situation and guiding them to the time that is available.

You have to realize most people are fairly flexible. They just want a massage. It doesn't matter if it is at 1 PM or 2:30 PM, and many times it's even okay if it's 1 PM on Wednesday instead of Tuesday. Often, they aren't familiar enough with what you do or your schedule to know what to ask for. They have made a decision to get a massage, and that's about as far as it goes. They have a time in mind, but it is an arbitrary one. It may be their day off, and they want their massage in the morning. While they may say they want 10 AM, if you can't do it 10 AM, they aren't going to hang up the phone in disgust when you offer them, "No, but I have a 10:30 AM available." They want a massage. They will be happier they got on your schedule more than they will be aggravated you wouldn't do it at the exact time they requested. Your existing clients will respond this way too, and you don't have to feel like you are going to lose them if you tell them you can't see them at a particular time.

Likewise, you must also remain flexible yourself, especially if you don't have a large client base. Just because you don't normally work on Mondays is no reason to decline the work on the grounds that it is your day off. If a person can only have a massage that day, you have to keep in mind she is willing to pay you and could become a regular customer. You never know who may call you. That Monday massage could easily turn into a client who comes religiously every week, so you aren't just declining $65 for the single massage, you're throwing away an opportunity to make over $3000 annually from that client. Plus, that client will be promoting your name as her massage therapist, and that can have an even greater impact on your business.

Sometimes there will be no possible way you can personally meet the needs of a person. Here's where your network of other massage therapists comes in again. You always have to keep in mind you are going to provide a solution no matter what. When you can't find an agreeable time in your own schedule, you quickly move to the next step. Your mentality needs to remain focused on the client in accommodating the caller. "Ask yourself how can I still meet their needs?" By offering alternatives, even if it means another therapist does the work, you put yourself in a position of authority. You are the one who made it happen, and the caller will be grateful. As your practice grows, more and more people will recognize this attribute about you, and your willingness to accommodate people will feed on itself. Because we never say no, our practice has grown to the point where we have had to hire employees. We became so booked we were constantly sending clients to other massage therapists, and while it may sound like an inconceivable idea to be so busy additional staff is required, we didn't begin our practice thinking that would be the outcome either. But, because we purposefully decided we would never reject an opportunity to give massage, our practice continues to grow, and so will yours.

The Art of Negotiating

There is a large gray area between yes and no. As we mentioned before, most people are more interested in getting a massage than they are in the exact time they receive it. This fact will always work to your advantage because you maintain control of when you schedule clients. It was hard for us in the beginning to offer another time, even if it were only thirty minutes earlier or later. We thought if we didn't do it at the requested time or the requested day, the person would hang up the phone. Once we realized we could still be in control of our business, we also began to take control of our schedules and we became more confident in our roles as business owners.

Knowing exactly when **you** can offer massage makes the entire process of scheduling easier on you. When we began our practice, we didn't have clients already in place, so if someone called and wanted 2 PM, and we would simply say yes because it wasn't like we were slammed with work. Then, we would get a call for someone who could only get a massage at 1 PM on the same day. Having already agreed to do a massage at 2 PM, we created our own conflicts because we had no set schedule for when we were prepared to start a session. We determined it was necessary to prepare our appointment books with designated times for massage appointments to better serve the client and maximize our output for the day.

We knew we were going to be in the office from 9 AM until 6 PM Tuesday through Saturday. That had already been established, but other than that, we confused being flexible with having an accommodating schedule. Even if you are just opening your practice, setting your schedule in advance gives you more leverage over how your days will transpire. If you are anticipating your practice to be your full-time occupation and plan on working forty-hour weeks, take your appointment book and circle 9:00 AM, 10:30 AM, (12:00 PM, 1:00 PM use one of these for lunch), 2:30 PM, 4:00 PM, and 5:30 PM. If you are currently working part-time, decide which days and what hours you plan on offering massage and circle them. Those times are your basic appointment times. And you'll probably fill your schedule more easily, if you take your lunch early and put 4 available slots in the afternoon. The full-time schedule gives you seven available appointments a day, and it doesn't matter if they aren't filled at first. When you know precisely when you will offer massage, you always allow yourself enough time to handle requests. For instance, if someone calls and wants 2 PM, you can immediately say, "No, but I have 2:30 PM." You don't have to try and figure out whether or not you can accommodate the exact request. You know in advance you begin your afternoon massages at either 1 PM or 2:30 PM, and you can tell the caller what you have available without hesitation.

You have to remember someone calling you on the phone can't see your schedule. She's not aware you have nothing at all scheduled on the day she wants. She just gave you the time that happened to come to mind or that was most convenient. By having set times every day, you control the conversation. Consider these two phone calls.

"Good Morning, This is Kneaded Energy, my name is Bill, How can I help you?"

"I'd like to schedule a massage for Friday."

"Yes, would you prefer morning or afternoon?
Afternoon would be better."

"Would you like 2:30 or 4:00?"

"Oh, four would be better for me."

"Okay, we'll schedule you for 4:00 on Friday."

With two direct questions, the client got what she needed. When people want something they are unfamiliar with, they want to be guided. They don't just want the actual service; they want the process to be simple and straightforward. Now, look at the alternative.

"Hello"

"Yes, is this the massage place?"

"Yes"

"I'd like to schedule a massage"

"Ok. When?"

"Oh, what do you have available on Friday?"

"I'm pretty open. Well I have to drop my car off."

"Do you have 3:00?"

"Well, no I have to leave by then."

"Well, ok, do you have anything at 1:00?"

"Oh, sure, I can do it then."

"At 1:00, for an hour and a half?"

"Uh, well, yeah, I could do that."

You put yourself at a disadvantage when the caller is expected to ask all the questions and guide you through the conversation. Booking an appointment should be organized and client centered – then it becomes easy. Your lack of assertiveness will come across as indecisive, disorganized, and unprofessional to the caller.

When you have your schedule predetermined, you stay in control of the situation. Even if you've got a client standing in front of you looking at your appointment book, you don't necessarily have to schedule a massage at the time requested. If you know ahead of time when you offer massage, it won't matter if a client is staring at your empty calendar. This scenario has happened numerous times to us. For example, a woman wanted to schedule a massage for the morning. On the appointment book, it looked like the entire morning was available, but it, in fact wasn't. We told her we could schedule her massage at 11:30 AM. She was confused by the lack of appointments earlier in the morning, but she didn't know the whole story. We had an off-site massage at 9:00 AM, which required travel time. There was no way we could have returned to be ready for anything before 11:30 AM. We simply marked out the other times, asked again if 11:30 AM would work. She scheduled at that time, and we remained in control of the situation. And we also maintained our professionalism as therapists. If we had agreed to an earlier massage, we would have had to rush the off-site session or been late to her appointment. Either way, we would have looked unprofessional.

There are exceptions to every principle. We have a regular client who gets a massage every Thursday at 4:00 PM. He's come in every week for two years. One day after his massage was over he asked if he could move his massage up to 3:30 PM. We said it was no problem, even though it messed up the early afternoon appointments. It made it almost impossible to give a 2:30 PM massage on Thursday, but that was fine. This particular regular client pays a good portion of our mortgage, and we knew attending to his simple request would be more advantageous over time than holding firmly to our regular afternoon appointment times. So, allow yourself to alter your "set" schedule in situations where you'll be better off in the long run. The point is, by creating a series of standard appointment times, gives you a great deal more control over how your practice operates.

Tell Your Clients What You CAN Do

Existing clients and prospective clients want to know what you CAN do for them. They don't want to know what you can't do for them. They don't really care why you can't give them a massage. They only want you to take care of their needs. Some massage therapists publish their limited and inconsistent office hours on brochures, business cards, and websites. What they believe is beneficial to their businesses is actually a distraction and a hindrance to building a practice.

When you publish your limited office hours, such as: Open - Monday, Wednesday, and Saturday 9-12 and 2-5, you're essentially saying no to anyone who was previously interested in Friday or late on Wednesday. If someone repeatedly sees your limited office hours, many times they will be remembering when you **don't** work, not when you do. You're advertising what you don't do.

It also is not necessary to advertise that you are still working another job to make ends meet. If you are in that situation, when someone wants a time when you are employed elsewhere, don't say you're not available because you are working your other job. You have to go back to the immediate response, "Yes, let's see, I have this available and that available", or "No, I'm booked at that time, but…." If you are still employed at another job and only work several days a week, keep track of and recognize when you begin to turn down people regularly because you are scheduled out for six weeks. Telling someone you can't see her because you are working your other job translates to "I'm not that good because I'm not that busy" and means she will go somewhere else. When you do this too many times, you have to ask yourself what you are giving up. If the ultimate goal is to be doing massage full-time, you must be acutely aware of the business you're throwing away because you keep explaining why you can't see more clients. The same is true for times when you are engaged in some other personal activity. It is completely unnecessary to tell a caller you can't see them because you are going to the doctor or taking your kids on a field trip. That is not necessary information. It is sufficient to say you don't have the first selected appointment available, but let me tell you what I do have available." If you're always prepared with an alternative solution, which will increasingly occur as you get busier, you'll never put yourself in a position of turning down paying clients.

> Saying "No, I'm booked at that time, but I have this available..." is concise, and covers a multitude of reasons, none of which are the client's business. It also takes some confusion out of doing business.

Knowing what you will say when a conflict arises with scheduling means you never have to sound like you are making excuses. It's difficult to learn to avoid this mistake because it's a very natural thing to "explain" your circumstances. "I'm booked at that time, but I have this other time" or "No, I'm booked at that time, but I can find someone to help you.", requires thought and consideration. It requires negotiation, but it's worth the effort. Many times massage therapists attempt to explain why there's a problem because they are afraid of angering the person wanting a massage. There's a sense that the client will "understand" **better** if they go into detail about why a time doesn't work. When you give reasons why you can't schedule someone, you're disrupting the scheduling process. You make the client work harder to find a time that does fit. Take the work away from the client. Make scheduling easy. Let your pre-set available appointments dictate scheduling and leave all the extra things going on in your life out of the equation. Saying "No, I'm booked at that time, but…" is concise and covers a multitude of reasons, none of which are the client's business. It's different than saying, "No, I'm not available then, but…." The former response suggests you have clients; the latter is merely ambiguous. It's a small nuance, but when you convey a positive "I'm busy with clients" attitude, the caller will be more apt to want to purchase what others have obviously already done with great satisfaction.

Other Problems with saying "No"

Saying no to events, paid or unpaid, is just as hard on your business as declining clients. If you've done a particular event in the past without much luck, and are asked to do it again, be extremely careful about saying no. Remember, the exact same people won't be in attendance, and it is another opportunity to be in front of the public. You may have to rework how you present yourself or what you offer, but when you say no, event planners will cross you off their lists of potential participants. Even when an event is unpaid, it is still a chance to gain exposure, and exposure, at no direct cost to you, is the simplest way to attract clients.

There may come a day when someone calls and asks you to teach a class or speak at a meeting. You may have never done it before and might be extremely uncomfortable at the thought, but you never know how it will impact your business in the future. We were asked to teach a class about business at a local massage school. We were worried and nervous because we had never taught a class before, but we did it anyway which lead to a world of opportunity. When you're requested to function as a massage therapist in any fashion, never say no emphatically. Always say yes and then work out the details. Always consider your affirmative answer as an investment in the overall direction of your business.

One other common scenario of when massage therapists say no is same-day bookings. We find this to be a contradiction to success. Here are the reasons. First of all, they think if they agree to a same-day massage, the person will conclude they aren't busy or successful. They turn down the paid work out of their own personal discomfort and need for control. People are spontaneous and impulsive. There could be any number of reasons why someone needs a massage that day, and turning him down is lost revenue. He won't assume, "Wow, she must be really busy." He'll think, "Well, I guess I won't call her again."

The second reason therapists turn down same-day massages has to do with the misperception about when they work. They see themselves as massage therapists only during massage sessions. If someone called to schedule an appointment at 4:30 PM, and because they had already decided their 2:30 PM appointment would be the last one of the day, they turn the client away. When you make yourself unavailable because you aren't interested in giving the massage at a specific time, you waste perfectly good opportunities with potential clients.

The way our schedule is set up, we have seven available spots for massage. Our goal is to do five massages a day. If we do those, we have met our requirements, but we have the other two appointments available for last minute calls. If someone hurts his neck or slips in the shower, we want to be able to take care of those immediate, unforeseen needs. We stay in the office until 6 PM regardless of our client load because people do call for same-day service. If we denied them a massage, or we didn't find another therapist to do it, we would be losing potential growth. It might just be that one massage, but it also might be the first stepping stone to a regular weekly client or an in-road to a large corporate event. You just never know.

Saying no to giving massage is never about the specific appointment. It's a bigger opportunity than you realize. Always find a way to accommodate the people who want your help. When you gain a reputation for never saying no, you'll find yourself in the very enviable position of having other massage therapists jealously asking you how you became so successful.

Chapter 7

Summary and Things to Consider

Principle 4: Never Say No

- Build a network of Massage Therapists you can rely on as backup when scheduling:
  - o Couples Massage,
  - o Vacation, Sick Leave, Maternity Leave,
  - o Personally I'm booked at that time, however, I have another massage therapist who can work with you.
- The art of negotiating.
  - o Instead of No, I'm booked, how about; Yes, but: "Yes we can schedule a massage, but I'm booked at 5 pm, how would 6:30 for you?"
  - o Instead of I don't work then, how about; Yes, however: "Yes we can schedule a massage, however I don't come into the office until 10 am that particular day, would 10:30 work for you?"
- Set a schedule in your workday.
  - o It's ok to book your day convenient for you based on 1-1/2 hour time slots.
  - o Book time in your schedule for laundry, marketing, returning phones calls.

Section III

Retaining Clients

Retaining Clients

Retaining the clients you already have is a vital component to a thriving private practice, yet many massage therapists approach retention in a completely backward manner. Many methods people use are ineffective because these tactics are more appropriate for attracting new clients rather than keeping existing ones. Conventional marketing wisdom tells us to saturate the market with our brand. We need to keep our names in front of the buying public, so in order to do that, we mail flyers, make phone calls, and send e-mail. All of these are good options in "branding" your business to the general public, however once they become a client, the nature of the confidential "therapist-client" relationship changes and massage therapists in private practice can no longer effectively use these strategies in the same way. Our occupation is unique in this way because our clients are not buying color TVs or tanning services. It is a very personal, private interaction, and bombarding them with marketing messages confuses the dimensions of that relationship. Massage therapy is not a market commodity; the nature of our work is hands-on, which gives us a unique responsibility to honor the therapist-client power differential.

We know this philosophy flies in the face of everything you have heard about how to retain clients and keep them coming in for more massages. Up until this point, we have told you to be aggressive in attracting potential clients, but when it comes to existing clients, there's a major shift that has to occur. We know this approach works though, so in reading this section, keep in mind the principles are long-term investments in the future profitability of your practice.

Retention is much easier than you think, but you have to make this shift in thinking about what it means. Essentially, we look at our clients as retaining us as massage therapists, not us retaining them as clients. As long as we remain in practice, we are their massage therapists. We continue to be the people they turn to for massage—whenever that may be. Retaining clients is a much more passive activity when you perceive it this way. Unless someone has had an absolutely horrible experience with you, most often she sees you as her massage therapist, regardless of how many times she comes to see you. She comes when she needs massage. It's really that simple. The frequency is not all too different than buying services from an electrician, a piano tuner or a psychotherapist. You wouldn't expect to hear from any other service provider on a regular basis. You determine when you go see them based on your needs. And if you've ever received a birthday card from your electrician, how heart-felt was that card sent and received? Did it really spur you to call and make an appointment to have your house rewired? When we, as massage therapists, bombard our existing clients with marketing, we are expressing **our wants**, not **their needs**.

> *Our clients retain us as their massage therapists. Not us retaining them as clients.*

We want them to come in more frequently because that means immediate cash, but as far as the lifetime value of a client goes, we are much better off in the long run to stay away from directly marketing to them once they have become clients. They will come because you are their massage therapist. Many massage therapists operate out a sense of fear of losing existing clients, and their methods for getting them to return often have the opposite effect. We're going to discuss the various attributes of passive and active retention. We do advocate marketing to clients, but it is in a very different manner than more popularly known strategies.

At the end of the day, you are doing many things to retain your clients without even knowing it. If you aren't getting what you would consider a lot of repeat business, changing the definition of how you view retention and repeat clients can have a tremendous eye-opening experience for you. When you stop chasing after the tactics that don't work, you will realize how much simpler the whole concept really is to achieve.

Chapter 8

Principle 5:

Once You Get Them, Leave Them Alone

"Your task is not to perform, it is to satisfy."

\- Harry Beckwith

Your main objective as a massage therapist is to achieve a level of business where most of your clients come in on a frequent and regular basis, right? Well, not really. Your job is to use your skills and knowledge of massage to fulfill the needs of your clients, regardless of their regularity. Their needs vary widely and encompass a whole range of definitions about when and how often massage is necessary in their lives. There's a common misunderstanding among massage therapists that if a client does not come in every week, she is not a good client. Massage therapists assume things about those infrequent customers. They think they didn't give a "good enough" massage to merit returning, or "Massage is wonderful, so clients should want it on a regular basis."

In most cases the job you performed was a very good one and extremely appreciated by the recipient, and it is unfair to yourself for you to "blame" your skill level or massage technique for the reason that person did not return the following week. Don't kick yourself; look at the bigger picture of how the service industry works. There could be financial reasons why someone only comes in once a quarter or once a year. She may only come in when she gets a gift certificate on her birthday or at Christmas. She may get a massage when her husband is away on a business trip. People's motivations for choosing massage are completely unknown except to them. As far as the second assumption goes massage is typically a good experience for all who receive it, but consider again how many times you personally got a massage before you went to massage school. And now that you're practicing and immersed in it, how many massages do you personally pay for now? In classes we've taught, 16 out of 20 students never received massage prior to school, 3 had it once or twice, and 1 got massage on a regular basis. Those numbers are fairly accurate for the general population too, so why would you believe that trend would reverse itself now that you are the one giving the massage?

Repeat massage clients are very much like repeat clients for many other businesses. Just because you love pizza, does that mean you order it every night? You may have found the best pizza place in the world, but, as the consumer, **you** determine how many times you buy it. Chances are if you have a favorite restaurant, you don't go around trying other places. When you want pizza, you look forward to the experience you will have as a result of getting it from **your** pizza place. If you consider service-related businesses, the same thing occurs. If **you** have a plumbing problem, you call a plumber. When he does a good job, you don't call for another visit the next week unless you have another plumbing issue. But, if three years down the road there's a problem, who are you going to call? The same plumber. Why? Because he is your plumber. It's too much trouble to find another "good" plumber, and all you will be thinking is how much you hope he's still in business with the same phone number and location. When people can't find a business quickly and easily, they assume it is no longer available to them.

As a massage therapist, you are in the same category. People call you when they have a need, and they hope you are still around. When you change your phone number or move your office, you're effectively making it impossible for those clients who don't come in often to find you. They would prefer not to find another therapist, but you basically force them to when they cannot reach you at the last known number. But, here's the trick about repeat customers. You wouldn't want your plumber to call you up to see if any of your other pipes had burst, and you wouldn't necessarily want the pizza joint to call and ask, "Aren't you hungry anymore?" Consumers of products and services want to control how and when they buy, but many massage therapists want to push massage on their existing clients out of their own need for income under the guise that they are concerned and want to stay in touch with their clients. Stay in touch by staying put in your location. Stay in touch by keeping the same company name and phone number. Stay in touch by advertising. Stay in touch by giving pro bono work at community events. Stay in touch by answering your phone when it rings. Stay in touch periodically, at least once a quarter, with a newsletter of "what's new at the practice".

Consider how you would react if your physician called you on the phone to inquire about the frequency of your visits to him. Wouldn't you be a little turned off if he wanted to know if you weren't feeling just a little bit sick and wanted to come in? It sounds ridiculous, doesn't it? If he sent you a weekly e-mail, wouldn't you quickly begin deleting the unwanted messages? You go to the doctor when you have a specific need, and it doesn't mean you don't value the service he provides or would even consider going anywhere else. In your mind, he's **your** doctor. He's not sitting in his office moaning about how you just aren't a good client because you aren't a hypochondriac. The dentist, the chiropractor, nor the auto mechanic are fuming about how you aren't a good customer because you don't send them enough of your business to satisfy their predetermined levels of acceptable revenue. But, who do you immediately think of the moment you get a cavity or a pain in your spine or a blown engine?

Redefining Good Clients

Massage therapists pick an arbitrary number of times a client should come see them to define them as good because the frequency of visits determines their revenue. For instance, valuing a weekly client at $65 per session for 50 weeks equals $3250 for the year. Well, ten clients like that would be $32,500, and twenty clients would amount to $65,000. That sounds really great if you're just starting out. $65,000 a year for twenty clients a week doesn't sound like a bad deal, but for the vast majority of massage therapists, this scenario just never happens. Only a small percentage of the population can afford weekly massages. Quantifying a client's value based on frequency doesn't take into consideration how that person views you between sessions and what she is saying about you to others. When someone feels the need for a massage, chances are she will not put it off, but individuals have very different ideas about when they do need it. For a small portion of the population, it is weekly, but the majority sees it as a monthly, quarterly, or yearly event. You can't worry about how often someone comes to your office, and it's unfair to devalue a client because he hasn't been to see you in a while.

A massage therapist asked us how many clients we had. At the time we said 2500, and then she asked how many were inactive, assuming we were trying to inflate our status because we had seen a lot of clients. We told her three were inactive.

She couldn't believe it, but we told her those three clients had died. At one point we did go through our files to try and make better use of our space, so we placed clients who hadn't been to see us in the last three years in a separate drawer. The week we did that two people from the supposedly "inactive" file called for massage because, for them, that's when they needed us. We've had the three clients we saw that first January we were open return to see us nearly four years later. While we assumed those people who had not been back to see us were lost forever, we were missing the important fact that we never stopped being their massage therapist. They were still <u>retaining us</u> as their massage therapists. We realized all clients should be considered active—no matter how frequently they come for massage. The reasons for the gaps between massages have nothing to do with the massage therapist; it's simply how clients view their personal needs and how their lives ebb and flow.

> *While we assumed those people who had not been back to see us were lost forever, we were missing the important fact that we never stopped being their massage therapist. They were still retaining us as their massage therapists.*

When we recognized the truth of this fact, it became much less worrisome when a client didn't schedule another massage for the upcoming week. We realized that although they may not have been supplying us with a steady source of revenue, we never stopped being their massage therapist. Any time massage therapy comes up in conversation, they refer to us as **their** massage therapist. It's an important distinction to go from the "my clients" mentality to the "their therapist" philosophy. When you are "their therapist," you don't have to do anything because it is a completely passive action. You just are who you are. By making this shift in thinking, you no longer have to quantify them by the amount of money they pay you, and you can refocus your attention on attracting new clients and being fully present for the clients on your table and returning to be on your table.

We have a client who came to see us once a year for three years, then she came in four times in two weeks because of an injury. In between all that time, she never went to see anyone else. It never occurred to her to consider another massage therapist because she came to us. But, it took work and consideration on our part as well. When the client got hurt, we could have responded by telling her our next appointment was six weeks out because our five each a day schedule was full. Remember though, we have the potential for seven appointments a day. Our average of five a day increased for the next two weeks and so did our income, but more importantly, we cemented our service in her mind. We consider her a regular client. Our job was to be available to her when she needed us, not to convince her she ought to get massage on a more regular basis. If we had sent her monthly reminders, she might have been turned off at the intrusion into the rest of her life and never come back. The frequency with which she came for massage had nothing to do with how attracted she was to us, though when we started our practice, that's what we naturally thought when a client didn't return for a long time. "Oh well, I guess we just didn't click," or "We didn't do something right for that person." We were concentrating on ourselves rather than on the client, and when that happened, we were making assumptions that just weren't true. In reevaluating who your active clients are, you have to believe and accept you will remain their therapist as long as you are in practice and easily accessible, even if they only come every two years. It's a very freeing experience when you stop worrying about what you did wrong or why Heather Smith hasn't been to see you in a while.

Discounting infrequent clients has a significant impact, and we became aware of how important they could be at Christmas. We send four regular marketing messages to our existing clients every year, once a quarter. It comes in the form of an e-mail, and it is a reminder about gift certificates. We found that many of the clients on our e-mail list would indeed come in and purchase gift certificates for presents, even if they had only been to see us themselves one time. One year a client asked all her family for gift certificates for massage. She received twelve gift certificates and came in once a month the next year. We were the massage therapists she used, but more importantly, she told twelve people to come to our office to buy gift certificates. Those people may have never gotten a massage from anyone in their lives, but who do you think they will think of now? Our client's Christmas request was a more effective marketing strategy than anything we could have done throughout the year to get her specifically to come in more often. It all stemmed from the fact that she made people aware of what she wanted because we reminded her **one time** about of our gift certificate program. The rest of the year we weren't counting or judging how many times she came to see us.

People who get regular weekly massage are far and few between. If we were counting on our weekly clients to support us, we'd have gone out of business a long time ago. Massage therapists make the mistake of believing if they could just get "regular" clients, they'd be set. This idea is similar to believing if only a chiropractor or a doctor would get a massage from you, then he'd send all his clients to you. There's simply no one source from which you can derive all your business. It doesn't work with complimentary businesses, and it won't work with regular clients. Seventy percent (70%) of your clients will see you 1, 2, or 3 times a year, so you are better off spending your time gathering up more and more of these seemingly irregular clients, instead of pestering the living daylights out of your existing client base. It might seem like a great way to operate your practice, but working on the same people week in and week out could get tedious because you are so familiar with them and what they want. While they are providing you steady income, you sacrifice some of the pleasure that comes from a variety of different people.

Active Passivity

No, this isn't an oxymoron. It is a very conscious decision. Retaining clients is both direct and indirect, but staying out of people's private lives is critical to retaining them. There are a number of ways to be Actively Passive. Clients see you as functioning in a single role in their lives—their massage therapist. When you step over that boundary, you are attempting to have a relationship that doesn't exist. Calling a client you haven't seen in a while and asking her how she feels and if she'd like to schedule a massage is intrusive. That's what friends do, and you aren't your clients' friend. Calling your scheduled clients to remind them of their massage is not necessary, unless you've made that part of your business plan. Following up with cards or e-mails to your clients need to be done carefully and tactfully. Don't assume a level of welcome outside the business setting even with these transactions. Be sure to always thank them in person. Actively decide not to make unnecessary contact. Actively choose to be passive. While it may sound crazy not to stay in contact with your clients (based on conventional marketing wisdom,) when you make the transition from possessing them as **your** clients to allowing them to define you as **their** therapist, it's easy to leave them alone.

Another simple way to be passive is to stay consistent. Get a phone number that will **never** change. Choose your office location very carefully and never move. Continue to go to the places where they saw you in the first place. Work the same events. Advertise in the same places. We make sure a client who hasn't been to see us in a long time leaves with a magnet to put of his fridge. Our clients know where we are; they see us when we do free events at their offices, and they see our advertisements. We don't need to call them up personally because we make sure they are continually exposed to our marketing efforts for potential clients on a regular basis. They are general, broad reminders that we are still in business. We are marketing to our target of prospects—not targeting our market of existing clients.

We explained in Chapter 5 the need to be repetitive when trying to gain access to a group. When members of that group become clients, your repetition must remain global in scope, not individual. Inundating existing clients with information about you and your business pushes more people away than it attracts. They don't want to hear from you every week or month because they aren't looking to be sold to. Don't send birthday cards to every client you see because it's inauthentic. Do you feel special when your bank sends you a birthday card? Twenty percent (20%) of your clients will appreciate the gesture, but the other eighty percent (80%) will be rolling their eyes because this tactic is so overdone it has lost any meaning. We don't suggest that you send blanket weekly e-mails either nor forward jokes to them. You can't assume that level of intimacy. The relationship changes when you become their therapist. You can be the most aggressive salesperson in the world until you get that person on your table, but once that happens, she is no longer a prospect.

In this business if you single out clients because they responded to general marketing you used to convince them to become clients, you cross a very serious threshold. What were once all-purpose sales and marketing pitches becomes intrusive, threatening, and coercive language. If you see an advertisement for a company in a magazine or on TV, you are reminded of your affiliation without feeling pressured. But, if a sales rep calls you directly, you're put in a position to make a decision under someone else's terms. When you continue to pursue broad active marketing strategies like advertising in publications, attending your chosen groups' events, and so on, you are passively speaking to existing clients without crossing that line. You can effectively keep your name in front of them without calling them up and saying, "I haven't seen you in three months. Would you like to schedule a massage?" The consistency with which you are in front of non-clients has a trickle down effect on existing clients without putting them on the defensive. Unfortunately, many massage therapists try to retain clients inappropriately and fail to get repeat business. Then, they get tired of spinning their wheels attracting new ones, and the combination of the two often leads to disillusionment, frustration, and even quitting altogether.

The Role of the Therapist

There are two roles a massage therapist plays. One we have already mentioned in the section on attracting clients. The active aggressive marketer has to be a part of how you achieve success, but an equally important role is the actively passive one you have once people become your clients. The manner in which you deal with the relationship you have with clients is crucial to retention. Both roles happen in conjunction with one another, but because active-aggressively pursuing existing clients turns a large majority of people off, you must immediately switch gears and assume the more actively passive role when it comes to marketing.

Many massage therapists aren't even aware that how they react to clients is the very reason why they don't come back. They send random e-mails that get no response, so they try the more direct route of calling clients. Each successive attempt on the part of the massage therapist only creates more dislike and distrust by the client. Clients take their names off of mailing lists and begin to screen calls because the relationship they have with the therapist is different than what the therapist thinks. Massage therapists have a much more intimate-but-removed relationship with their clients than a hair stylist or an electrician, and due to that relationship, you have an ethical obligation other service providers don't have.

Consider the business of a psychotherapist. He needs to get his name in front of potential clients to stay in business, but when someone makes the decision to come in and discuss personal problems, the psychotherapist can't then call the client up and ask when he wants to come back in and talk some more. It is breaking a trust, and it is going beyond the arena where that relationship has been established. The massage therapist is no different. Instead of psychological issues, you're dealing with the physical element of touch. You can't presume to have access to your clients' private lives. Furthermore, you shouldn't presume to have access to them outside your office. You may be a very important person in their lives because of what you provide them, but you remain, in their minds, an individual to whom they pay for specific services. And that's all. For this reason, it is never a good idea to attempt to get friends and family to become clients. The power differential should always remain very clear, and people you are familiar with outside of your life as a massage therapist muddy those roles.

This concept of being passive is sometimes very hard to do, and we've made many mistakes along the way. When a person comes to you for massage, the relationship you have with him is exclusively within the confines of your office. It doesn't mean you can't ever speak to a client unless he's lying on your table, but you always have to honor the therapist-client relationship. We acknowledge but never initiate conversations with clients we see in other places like the grocery store or a health fair. If they want to talk to us, that is perfectly fine, and we respond accordingly, but we have no idea whether our clients talk publicly about their trips to us. There are many clients who don't want others to know they get massage. If we initiated a conversation in a public place by asking how a client's back was feeling, she might be embarrassed or angry or offended. We just don't know. You always should let your clients dictate conversation.

Massage therapists believe massage is a very wonderful and pleasant experience, and so every encounter with a client should have the same kind of feeling. When a client thanks you for the service you provide, that is not an invitation to enter her life and come to dinner or go out and have a drink. You have to remember you are being paid to do one thing, and when the massage is over, so is the relationship with that client until the next massage. It's impossible to recreate that relationship in the grocery store aisle, even if a client wanted you to. The relationship you have is warm, personal, and private. Sales letters, flyers, random e-mails are cold and anonymous and come across as appearing desperate. There is no way to take your relationship and stuff it into an envelope. There's no way you can even take it to the parking lot because what you do for clients happens inside the office.

We feel very strongly about keeping the relationship clear between us and our clients. A client had a session with one of our employees. It was the last one of the evening, and the client paid, rescheduled, and left. Our employee closed up the office and was in the parking lot when the client came back around the corner in his car. He rolled the window down and explained he had forgotten to tip our employee. She told him "not to worry about it" because essentially that relationship interchange was over for the day. It is impossible to extend the reach of that relationship beyond the office setting. The client did not mean to do anything wrong, and, in fact, he was doing what he thought was the proper thing to do, so it isn't always the therapist who acts inappropriately. We do want this issue to be clear. There are many clients who don't know how to act with regard to their relationship with their therapist, so it isn't always the therapist's fault, but as the therapist, the person in power, the dominant person in the relationship, you often have to guide them by your own actions. Our employee had her boundaries clear in her mind and explained to the client they could take care of the tip at his next massage. She wasn't harsh or abusive with him, but in an effort to keep that line clearly drawn, she had to educate the client about where their relationship began and ended.

Because we don't have any clue who else knows about our relationship with a client, we know that sending cards and making phone calls can hole a lot of risks. There are a lot of variables to keep track of and a lot of room for error. If you are going to use this tool, use it wisely. Make sure you get all the information and permission from the client upfront. Which phone line is confidential? Which email address is private? We decided the potential repercussions were not worth the trouble because it only takes one breach of that privacy to cause serious problems. It has paid off for us because we've been in business long enough to realize our clients will return to us when they have a need, not when it would financially benefit us. If you don't have a full schedule of clients yet, you will be better off using your time to attract new clients than going uninvited into the lives of the ones you have. The confidentiality and ethics are really no different than those that bind doctors and patients. While massage therapists aren't currently regulated by the same guidelines as physicians, we should still maintain that same standard. It is fundamentally important to maintain the integrity of that relationship.

We're open to conversations with our clients outside our office, and most of our clients do come up and speak to us, but we never want to put someone in the position of having to explain who we are when he doesn't want to. It can happen so fast, and you won't even realize you'd said something your client would rather keep private. Before you know it, you've created a problem. Sometimes it doesn't have any lasting effects, but it could mean that client never comes to see you again. You just never know how comfortable someone is about the relationship he has with you outside the office. When you see clients in public places, you are not doing yourself a favor by putting them on the spot. There's no way you can magically transform the office setting anywhere else simply by asking how someone is feeling. We ask for phone numbers and permission to call, but it is only for an emergency on our end where we are unable to do the massage at the scheduled time, not to create a database of contacts to call in the event we feel business is a little too slow.

There are many massage therapists who probably use some of these marketing tactics frequently with no ill effects, but we made a conscious decision to refrain from such strategies, and it has benefited our practice. By allowing our clients to retain us as their therapist and to control their own needs without our uninvited intrusions into their private lives, we can concentrate on building our practice through new clients and focus our attention on the people we work on. When you can let your existing clients come as they see fit, you also establish a stronger professional profile for yourself and your practice. As far as marketing to her outside the office, being passive once a person has become a client will give you more credibility. That existing client base may not come to see you any more frequently, but you have kept their trust and maintained the integrity of the relationship. It is often the things you don't do that have the biggest impact on clients' minds.

In the next two chapters, we will explain the active sides of retention, and how to maximize your position with existing clients. Active doesn't mean aggressive, and it doesn't mean over the top and fake. By staying out of clients' lives and employing the principles in the following chapters, you will be retaining your clients, and you'll realize how much simpler it is when you utilize the proper strategies.

Chapter 8

Summary and Things to Consider

Principle 5: Once you Get Them, Leave Them Alone

- People call when they have a need.
- Consumers of products and services want to control how and when they buy.
- Stay In Touch with Your Clients, by:
  - o Staying in the same location
  - o Keeping the same phone number
  - o Keeping the same business name
  - o By advertising
  - o By doing pro bono work in the community
  - o By answering your phone
  - o Keeping office hours

Chapter 9

Principle 6:

Practice Unconditional Positive Regard

> *"Be Mindful.*
> *Take a moment to let go of your inner dialogue*
> *and appreciate your immediate surroundings.*
> *Simply notice the sights and sounds and*
> *appreciate the quiet openness of the moment."*
>
> ~ Michael Carroll

Carl R. Rogers first coined the term "unconditional positive regard" in the early 1960s as one of the requirements by which a therapist must meet his client. Rogers was a psychotherapist who developed a completely different approach to treating psychological problems, and it was based on the idea that the therapist should not let his own interests get in the way of a patient's progress. Initially, he called this methodology "non-directive" because he felt like it was the therapist's responsibility to avoid guiding the patient to discovery. Then, he renamed his approach to "client-centered," which basically meant the same thing, but his goal was to allow the patient recognize and understand solutions without interference.

This philosophy, originally designed for the psychological realm, is equally applicable to that of massage therapy and retaining clients. Rogers believed there were three requirements a therapist needed to be effective—congruence, empathy, and respect, or unconditional positive regard.

> *Rogers believed there were three requirements a therapist needed to be effective—congruence, empathy, and respect, or unconditional positive regard.*

Congruence simply means being honest and authentic with yourself and with the client, and in doing so, you do not force the client to deny anything about them. You allow the whole person to be part of a session. There are many situations where people are self-conscious about themselves for one reason or another, and if you act like it doesn't exist, you show your own distaste or discomfort by your silence. For instance, if a client is severely overweight, you don't need to pretend it doesn't exist, especially if their weight hinders the therapy session. That means if it is necessary to ask the person to move his stomach away from the upper thigh to work a hip attachment, you do it as naturally and comfortably as if you were asking a client to turn over on to his back. The client knows he's overweight, and your honesty about it shows that you are concerned about giving him what he needs, regardless of his body type, shape or differences. Openness leads to trust, and when your clients trust that you have their best interests at heart, they will be more inclined to continue coming to get massage. Trust is a 2-way street that allows open and interactive communication, both verbal and non-verbal.

Empathy is the ability to feel what the client feels. When someone explains to you what is happening with his body, you hear and understand what he's trying to express. Rogers, in his therapy sessions, practiced a technique called "reflection." When a person said something, his reply was designed to let the patient know he was listening. For instance, if a patient exclaimed, "I feel like crap!" the therapist would reply with, "So, things aren't going so well for you lately, huh?" In massage, listening and truly understanding what someone is telling you about what you're doing are the only ways to know if you are meeting his needs. So, when a client tells you you're using too much pressure, you reply and show your empathy manually by applying less pressure.

Another way to keep a personal closeness to what your clients feel is to continue to receive massage yourself from a therapist you trust and respect. As you become more and more practiced at giving massage, the first thing you lose is the ability to remember what that initial touch feels like. You are touching backs and legs and shoulders all day long, week after week, and it's easy to forget what the physical reaction feels like for the client. You disregard the impact out of familiarity. Even after all the years we've been in practice, we still go to other therapists to get massage, so we keep fresh in our minds what our clients are experiencing when they are with us. When you are closely attuned to the experience you're giving, you'll have a greater appreciation and ability to address a client's requests.

Respect, or unconditional positive regard, is the ability to allow clients to be who they are without bias or judgment from you. No matter how you may feel personally about an individual it is your job as a massage therapist to enter a session professionally and with acceptance of who that person is. It is very difficult to do because we all have our own personal history we cannot throw away. We all have something to overcome, but we can only do so successfully if we are prepared beforehand to do so. Our own hang-ups run the gamut of physical, emotional, and moral opinions, but if you let your difficulty with a particular situation enter into a massage, your client will sense it through your hands. Many times you may be completely unaware of an aversion you have until someone is on your table, then it is too late. When the time for action arises – the time for preparation is past. When you go ahead with the massage thinking how utterly repulsed you are, you will not be able to give that person everything they need. Being able to give unconditional positive regard must be something planned prior to stepping into the room because your anxiety or discomfort with a certain kind of person will be a subconscious reaction.

We all dislike some kinds of people for one reason or another, but, as a massage therapist, if you let that enter into a session, you will probably see that client only once. The irony of having personal issues with certain types of individuals is they will be the very clients you attract and who respond to your marketing efforts. But, when you are not able to give them what they need because of fear or repulsion, you effectively kill your chances of retaining them. When you accept them for being overweight or old, uncommunicative or bizarre, they will appreciate your authenticity and concern and will consider you the therapist they turn to for massage.

There are an infinite number of settings where you might find yourself unable to satisfy the needs of a client. Ultimately, you must ask yourself, "Why does this bother me?" Are you uncomfortable with obese clients because you are fearful you may not find the muscles? Does an elderly woman remind you of your grandmother who recently passed away or are you afraid you'll hurt them? Are you uncomfortable when someone wants to talk to you or uses their cell phone during a session? Are you bothered when someone doesn't want to interact at all? Whatever the dislike or discomfort may be, in order to give unconditional positive regard, you must ask yourself what about the situation bothers you so much. It is imperative to discover what makes you uncomfortable and realize and understand why it crossed your boundaries. You have two choices. You can deal with it emotionally or accept the impossibility of getting over it. Your discomfort is **never** the client's problem. You have to own it as your own problem. If you can recognize the underlying reason, the next time the situation occurs you will be prepared to avoid bringing it into the session with you. Better yet, take the time now to contemplate your potential issues, deal with it and put it behind you. If not, you're going to have clients whose needs are not met by you, and who might interpret that as unprofessional behavior, which will have serious ramifications to your reputation.

In addition to physical eccentricities like obesity, deformity, and disease, you may have clients who are morally offensive to you. They might curse frequently, profess to be an atheist, or be gay. If it bothers you and you let it enter your session, you will be judging them with your hands. Does someone's personal behavior or attitude make a difference in the service they've asked you to do for them? It shouldn't, but this is why it is so challenging to realize what bothers you and leave it at the door. Unconditional positive regard is a state of mind you carry with you everywhere you go, with every client. You can be as opinionated and adamantly opposed to a particular thing all you want until you walk into that room. Then, if it is your intention to give him what he needs, you cannot bring your own baggage with you.

Eliminating baggage from your life is not easy, and we aren't qualified to assist anyone in that process. You should

PRACTICE UNCONDITIONAL POSITIVE REGARD

only consult a licensed psychologist or psychotherapist for help with this. But through our experience, including psychotherapy, we've realized how critical for our own well-being it is that we can recognize what it is about ourselves that is creating the discomfort. Through operating our practice, we've discovered the impact unconditional positive regard can have on retaining our clients. Not all massage schools are equipped to teach these skills either. You spend the majority of your time learning technique and anatomy. It can be an eye-opening experience when you enter the real world of clients, their needs and their differences.

You will have situational issues too that can cause you to be unable to give unconditional positive regard, and unless you are willing to deviate from the near perfect setting in which you learned massage, you won't satisfy the needs of your clients. Bill's first client out of school was from a different country, doing business here in the United States. "When I returned to the room to begin the massage, the client was lying on the table in a full body suit. I wasn't prepared for that. With the exception of chair massage, I'd only been taught to perform massage on skin. There were really two routes to go with this client. I could have requested he take off the body suit, so I could be comfortable, to which he probably would have simply gotten up and left. Or, I could recognize the issue was my own, and I could give him a massage with the body suit on. I chose to modify my approach, but it certainly was unsettling because in order to give a good massage I was "supposed" to do it on bare skin. People do seemingly strange things, but they aren't unusual to them. While I initially considered the body suit a problem and a hindrance, the client believed it was an excellent alternative to keeping his regular clothes on. He was asking me to give him a massage on his terms, and that's really what every client does." When you can give unconditional positive regard, then you are allowing those sometimes bizarre terms to dictate the direction of the massage without your opinion affecting the situation.

A "proper" massage gets many massage therapists in trouble. What is a proper massage anyway? And furthermore who is a "proper" massage client? Is it a person who remains silent the entire time, so you can concentrate? Is it a person who accepts whatever you chose to do to them because you are the therapist in charge? Is it someone who isn't too fat or too old or too hairy or too smelly? Is it someone who responds positively to your supplementary products? A "proper" massage is the one inside your scope of practice that the individual client needs, and if you dictate to him what massage you want to give, you are demanding he abide by your set of rules and boundaries. By accepting who they are, you effectively take yourself out of the equation. They came to have **their** needs met, not yours.

Another common example of a situational conflict involves the issue of conversation. Some massage therapists don't want their clients to speak at all because they believe the massage has a better effect if performed in silence. The client can relax. You can concentrate. Being unresponsive to a client who is attempting to tell you about her children's sports team or the latest national news will make her feel like you don't care about her. She wants to engage in conversation throughout the massage because that is part of the experience and process to her. Conversely, other therapists believe clients should be as interested in their conversation as they are in the massage. Be flexible, but let the client lead in how much conversation will be entertained. If your client is lays on the table wishing you'd shut up, then you're going to have a very hard time convincing them to return. Why do you feel the need to enforce silence or conversation from your clients? When you can answer that question truthfully, you usually have to admit it is because it's what **you** need. The minute you begin trying to satisfy your own needs through your clients you're communicating loud and clear, this is my session.

We have clients who enjoy a very active conversation where they tell us personal information about their families and lives. Then, we have others we know absolutely nothing about beyond their massage requirements, and they have no desire to know anything about us. We also have clients who keep their cell phones on during sessions. One client, a small business owner in the service industry, keeps the phone right next to her, and when it rings, we turn down the music and wait before continuing the massage. She answers it as if she were at work because that's the message she wants to deliver. If we didn't allow all these clients to dictate how they wanted their sessions to go, they would look elsewhere. We had a client come to us from another therapist. She said, "I like you much better because you don't talk my ear off", it really had nothing to do with the actual massage. We give each client the permission to talk or not talk. It doesn't matter to us because we accept those needs without judgment.

You may be thinking, "Well, I'd never offend any client by objecting to a physical attribute or a personality trait." Think about a time when you felt some aversion to a client once they were on the table. The client may have never seen your facial expression or read your mind, but have you ever asked yourself why some clients never come back to you? Did you manually do anything wrong? Probably not, but you may have inadvertently sent them a message that you were uncomfortable. It happens so quickly and effortlessly unless you are constantly thinking about the needs of the client and not your own.

Shelley had a client who was extremely hairy. "Prior to entering the room, I would never have articulated an aversion to excessive hair, but when I undraped his back, I gasped. When I made the first pass down his back, my hands were covered with hair. I shuttered. I couldn't help it. At the time I didn't think it was an issue. I wasn't prepared to be bothered, and in failing to acknowledge this fact about myself, I was unable to give him what he needed because all I could think about was how freaked out I was about all that hair. In doing so, I let my personal issue distract me from doing what he'd asked me to do." Clients seldom warn you of their unique characteristics, and none of your clients will ask you, "Are you bothered by warts?" or "Is my weight going to be a problem for you?"

We could easily do every massage the same way. We call it "the dance." We were taught how to do that. Massage school teaches you how to conduct a massage. If you were lucky, you learned when a technique is most advantageous. When someone calls and asks for massage, it would be much simpler to do the same routine each time. "You want massage? Here's your massage. I'll do my dance." But, you're not selling a prepackaged product. Massage isn't a can of beans or a leaky faucet.

The same is true for clients who want you to do things you wouldn't technically consider massage but still falls within your "scope of practice". Bill has a client with Fibromyalgia. She asked Bill to massage her skin so lightly she wanted it to feel as if she had no muscles. "As far as massage training goes, it wasn't really part of any technique, but I never judged her requests on the basis of my personal need to perform massage as I had been taught. I gave her the freedom to tell me what she needed because, for her, that was massage. I could have attempted to explain she was wrong-headed about her definition of massage and gone ahead with my normal routine, but I would have been operating out of my own need and comfort level, not her need to explain what she wanted and needed from me."

This same client won a free massage from another massage therapist, and she asked me to call the therapist and explain what to do. I agreed to talk to the therapist prior to her scheduled appointment, but the therapist arrogantly told me that wasn't what **he** did. He said the light skin brushing wasn't massage. She decided to attend her free massage, and the therapist did "his dance." He did the massage he wanted to do. She returned to us the next week and said she'd never go to another therapist again because no one else would listen to how critically important it was to her health to be able to modify the amount of pressure given and allow her the freedom to express her needs and determine her own outcome. "By giving her unconditional positive regard, she became fully comfortable to develop trust with me, simply because I gave her permission to participate in the massage, instead of demanding she accept my style or version of massage.

As massage therapists, we are in that interesting class of service providers. Typically when an individual wants a service, it is because they have a problem they can't solve on their own. They want the service provider to fix it. For a leaky faucet, a plumber has certain methods by which faucets are fixed. The plumber doesn't need to ask the homeowner **how** he'd like it fixed, if it leaks rapidly or slowly, or when the problem first began. He simply does what he does to fix leaky faucets, and the homeowner is happy.

Just because you are licensed to practice massage doesn't mean you can automatically issue a solution based on a set of techniques. The service is too intimate and personal. Whether a client wants massage for reduction or elimination of pain or for pampering and luxury, she has a tactile connection to whether or not the massage therapist is actually fulfilling the need. A massage client asks for a massage, but every person has a different definition of what that means. A massage therapist cannot respond by saying, "If I give you a Swedish massage, your needs will be satisfied" and be 100% sure that technique will indeed fulfill the need. The client might very well benefit from a Swedish massage, but because she has her own set of physical and emotional needs and has a certain idea about what she'd like to see happen, you can't guarantee one particular technique will achieve that goal.

When you present your theory on what a client needs as the only way to attain that objective, you are not practicing unconditional positive regard. You are not honoring her ability to express her needs; you're simply exerting your own opinion and control without client consideration. In the long run, that mentality is more apt to turn people away. We have clients who request full body-no feet, full body-no head and face, back only, arms and legs and back, stomach and viscera, skin only, no skin — work through the sheet. Do you begin to see how different they are from each other, how unique? Meet you client in all their glory and practice unconditional positive regard. It's essential. When you can respect and honor the desires of a client, even if you don't like the person or believe you are doing massage or whatever, you're making a dramatic impression on the client.

Rogers believed people are naturally drawn to positive regard, and when you give it unconditionally, people recognize it subconsciously. If someone's obese, it's hard enough to comprehend removing your clothes for massage. If you give unconditional positive regard, he will appreciate your acceptance of him. The same is true for any physical difference or abnormality. No one wants to take their clothes off and worry about what the therapist thinks of them. By allowing all your clients the freedom to be themselves, they will be drawn to you in very strong ways. The flipside of giving unconditional positive regard is you benefit as well. When you release the baggage you have about a particular circumstance, you are lighter and have more self-acceptance.

Being present, facing one's fears, judgments, opinions and aversions can be a very tough challenge because they are usually deeply embedded in the psyche. Learning how to give unconditional positive regard to each person you see takes time and a personal dedication to understanding oneself, but the benefits to your practice are immeasurable. It requires "being present", to your client. A man from our wise counsel says: "The whole person who works as a therapist has to decide what part of his/her self comes into the room. Choose wisely." Emotional health is a critical component to providing clients with what they need from you. You aren't always going to be grounded before a session. Massage therapy is a job as well as a career, so you'll sometimes go into sessions just after you've gotten over the flu, returned from vacation, finished your ninth massage for the day, or had an argument with your spouse. But, when you are conscious of where you are and what your obligation to your clients are, you can recognize your external personal circumstances as being outside the boundaries of the relationship between you and the client and leave them outside the treatment room. Or immediately recognize, stop and ground yourself. Be present to your clients. Regardless of what has immediately happened to you, you can begin a massage wholly focused on the client on your table without carrying your personal life in with you.

The fact is, while the client may not be aware of all the protocols and procedures. She is well aware of how she wants to feel. If you can't give someone that very specific thing, then she will be disappointed. The only guide you really have to ensuring you have done what the client wanted is to know prior to the start what that is. We ask every client, "How do you want to feel when you get off the table?" In asking this question, we relinquish our stranglehold on the direction of the massage and allow the client the freedom to express the particular needs. We have no idea how anyone wants to feel, and we can't presume that each client will feel that unique way just because we rubbed her back, then her legs, then her arms, then her shoulders. Because the individual is unique, and life is different each and every day, the massage must be unique. By giving unconditional positive regard, we go into each session wholly concentrating on the client's needs, however odd or unusual they may seem to us.

Listening to what clients say and then fulfilling those requests without judgment are the most effective ways to retain them. In contrast to the passive method for retention from the previous chapter, retaining clients by practicing unconditional positive regard is active in the sense that you are providing clients with exactly what they are asking you to do. Through listening and the actual massage, you are actively retaining them with your hands. You don't have to worry about calling them or pressuring them to reschedule because with every pass you make, you're saying, "My only objective is to conduct this massage so you feel the way you want to feel." When you do this with unconditional positive regard each and every time, you will be a magnet, and clients will want to return for a repeat experience.

Chapter 9

Summary and Things to Consider

Principle 6: Practice Unconditional Positive Regard

- Your discomfort is never the client's problem.
- Eliminate emotional baggage from your life. Emotional health is a critical component to providing clients with what they need from you.
- They came to have their needs met, not yours.
- Listen to what the client says and fulfill those requests within ethical reason, without judgment.

Chapter 10

Principle 7:

Massage is Bigger than the Hour

"I knew instinctively that my life had changed forever.
I dimly sensed that it might be up to me
whether the change would turn out good or bad."

~ Bo Lozoff

For most people massage is an event. It may be regular and frequent, or it may be sporadic and occasional. The one thing it is not is a single hour of the day. Recall we mentioned in Principle #4 about never say no and that massage is bigger than the hour? Massage therapists tend to view clients by their timeslots in an appointment book, but for the client the massage is the whole experience. It reaches in both directions beyond the hour spent on the table. There is anticipation before the massage, before ever booking the massage, regardless of how often someone comes to see you. That mental build-up of anticipation and experience cannot be discounted simply because you can't see them when they call. It's like planning a mini-vacation, right now. Likewise, after the massage, clients have physical and emotional aftereffects, long after you have touched them. From the minute they call to schedule through the 4 weeks of waiting to the actual time of the massage and until they walk back out the door, you should conduct yourself in a manner that reaches beyond the skin and the muscles to that place in your clients' memories where you imprint the experience with your indelible mark as their massage therapist and all the reasons why they should return to you. The effects of the physical massage will eventually wear off, but if you create an environment, both before and after the massage, of a purely positive experience, you will retain far more clients than you will with the most enticing flyer, the most heartfelt phone call, or the sincerest follow-up e-mail.

The principles of "Live your business" and "Never say no" come back into play when people call you for massage, and while it doesn't matter if the person is a new client or an existing one, your existing clients have certain expectations about what they want. The initial phone call is obviously critical to getting the business, so when you are practicing massage full time, and you keep regular business hours, you will be there to receive the call. Your clients expect you to answer the phone, and when you do, there's a sense of relief in knowing they can take care of their business without hassle. The same is true when you figure out a way to accommodate their needs, even if you don't conduct the massage yourself. When those clients call you, they are looking for one thing—to schedule that massage. It goes beyond phone etiquette and a pleasant voice. The method by which you schedule repeat customers sends as strong a message to them as what you do while they are on the table. It says, "I'm here for you no matter what," and they will appreciate your attention and be all the more eager to arrive.

It's important to remember: for a client, the massage truly is bigger than the hour and begins when she knows the date and time of her massage. She will think about it for several days; she might tell her co-workers the day of the massage how excited she is, and her drive to your office will be full of thoughts of how wonderful it will be. You set the tone from the outset about where that person's mind is in relation to you. Accommodating her needs when she calls elevates your position in her mind because you want her thinking two things about you—one, you're easy to work with, and two, the massage is going to be exactly what she needs and wants. When you, as the massage therapist, think of your clients' massages as beginning when the phone rings, you expand your reputation exponentially beyond what your hands can do alone. If your clients believe they can always get in to see you, they will be more likely to reschedule, especially when they only get massage every once in a while. Difficulty in the buying process is the quickest deterrent to future purchases.

If scheduling the massage over the phone is the beginning of the massage, the moment a client enters your office is the culmination of that anticipation. Your client has now arrived, and in a short time, she will enter that stress relieving, magical luxurious state of massage. The preparation on your part to set the mood goes beyond your décor and smile. As the massage therapist, don't adopt the bad habit of "here's another massage". You have to keep present in your mind that this upcoming event is unique and special to the client's daily life. There's no getting around the fact that massage is far more familiar to you than it is to your clients, so treating them with an appropriate amount of concentrated attention only prepares them further for the hour they will spend lying on your table. If this sounds a bit elementary and unnecessary, there are many massage therapists who fail to view the times before and after a massage with the proper degree of importance when it comes to retention. In some practices the therapist has only the interaction of the touch-time – the intake/welcome and outtake/thank you, is handled by someone other than the therapist. It's all too easy to herd one client after another in through the gate, perform a massage, and send them on their way without ever recognizing the subtle impact and the seemingly inconsequential actions you have on a client's unconscious approval and desire to return.

The communication between therapist and client is the active precursor to the massage. More clients than you might expect have a very warped view of what massage is all about. They have images in their heads from television of a luxury hotel spa-like experience of massage on the beach. For newcomers, the only thing they can think of is what exactly taking off their clothes means. We discovered very early on how little our new clients understood about what to do and what they were allowed to do once they were actually in our office. We have had clients lying naked on top of the sheet when we reentered the room. We've had some remain fully clothed and seated. We've had some who were not sure what clothing they should take off. We decided it was imperative to the rate of retention to provide an overall positive experience by giving clients all the information they would need before they thought to ask. Being fully aware of a process allows someone to relax and be completely comfortable for the duration of their massage.

Intake: Record Your Clients' Personal Information

We are well aware every state has different requirements and regulations for massage therapists. Some states have no guidelines whatsoever, but regardless of the laws in your particular state, more pertinent documentation is **always** better for you and the client. In the appendix, you will find a copy of our **Confidential Client Information Form**, and we encourage you to use it and adapt it to your state rules if necessary. Not only will it give you some protection from possible lawsuits and legal wrangling, it will provide unparalleled notes for you to use in future massage for your clients.

When a client comes in for the first time, we require them to complete the 2 part-first page, which includes personal data, the objective of the massage, current condition, including relevant medical problems, and informed consent. The informed consent puts everything on the table upfront, so the client has no confusion about the role of the therapist or of the nature of the massage. When he signs and dates this page, it goes on file and is kept safe and confidential. The second sheet gives the client the opportunity to update any necessary health information and to designate which areas he would like worked on and what the focus of the massage should be for that specific session. We will discuss the bottom half of the form later.

When the top half has been filled out, we start asking questions. If someone has circled the lower back, we might ask, "When does it hurt." "Is there a particular time of day this hurts more than others?" "What causes the pain?" "When it hurts, what do you do to make it feel better?" "How do you sleep?" "Where is your TV positioned in relation to your chair?" "What repetitive task do you do at work?" All the questions help us figure out what the client needs because generally he is only under the impression he will be getting a massage, not necessarily a certain technique. When you list the types of massage within your scope of practice, most clients will assume they must choose one, as if they were buying a cell phone plan. A client might tell us he wants a Swedish massage because of the description on our brochure, but when we sit down prior to the session and ask questions, he might reveal a certain specific pain in her neck. Had we not asked questions about what he wanted, the Swedish massage technique would not have addressed all his needs. This is the moment you get to release "your dance" and meet the client with what they need.

The same goes with a massage therapist's style. One of the questions on the intake form addresses a client's previous experience with massage. If he indicates he's had a bad experience before, we want to know more details. If he says another therapist made him aggravated or uncomfortable by being very wooden and uncommunicative, we know he would prefer a certain degree of conversation. When you don't get more information than, "I want a massage," you are risking the possibility of not meeting a client's full set of needs—both physically and emotionally. Since each person will be different in what they like, dislike, want, and don't want, it is crucial for you to have as thorough an understanding of those needs before you begin. It's like meatloaf. It could be a fantastic meatloaf, but it all depends on what a good meatloaf is to you. Ask questions. Encourage descriptions and explanations.

Our initial question is always, "How do you want to feel when you get off the table?" The rest of the conversation stems from the client's response. This short interview takes about five minutes, and it isn't stealing time from the client. On the contrary, it is one of the most important steps to retaining her as a client. If we don't give her what she needs, regardless of her ability to articulate it, she will continue her search for a massage therapist who will address those needs. It's never good when a client leaves your office thinking, "That was good, but...." Once we have a direction to go with the massage, based on the client's explanation of her needs, we follow with a short, memorized, rehearsed speech we go through to explain what will take place when I leave the room, return and proceed with the massage. Some of you might think a speech is too limiting or canned, or sounds too rehearsed, but we do this for a couple of reasons. First, we are required to get the client's informed consent. This means we are required to tell them what we plan to do based on their described needs and they agree to the plan. Secondly, we have realized and adapted over the years a basic, rehearsed, instructional speech, to give the client all the information she needs to feel comfortable about what is about to take place over the next hour. This "speech" also acts as protection for us. If someone were to accuse us for improper behavior or something equally frivolous, we know we can bring in our client base who will testify that we basically say the same basic thing to every client. In our litigious society, overcompensating for a misunderstanding will be in your best interest. We include it here as a guide only, but we do know how significant an impact it has on preparing a relatively new massage client to our procedure. We'll explain some of our choice of words, afterwards.

The Speech

"I'll leave the room and let you get undressed and get on the table. Just get undressed to the level you're comfortable. Some people like to leave their underpants on; (use hand gestures) some people like to take them off. It doesn't matter to me. Just get under the top set of sheets (open the sheets) and start face down. All the important parts stay covered by the sheet. When I come back in the room, I'll put a pillow under your ankles. I'll uncover your back and work your back down to about the middle of your hips (use hand gestures), and then I'll work the back of your legs. I'll get you to turn over and slide down. I'll work with your feet and then the front part of your legs, then your hands, arms, shoulders, and then finish the massage working the top part of your chest (use hand gestures), your head, neck, and face. During the massage you can be as quiet as you like or as talkative, but massage is not supposed to hurt you in order to help you. So, if I do anything that causes you pain or discomfort, please let me know. I'll stop and check in. Do you have any questions?"

The purpose in being so specific in giving this information prior to leaving the room is first time clients don't know what to expect. If someone has never received massage before, or never had a table massage, she is probably a bit anxious about what she's about to do and confused about what she's supposed to do. When you can eliminate the stumbling blocks of anxiety and vulnerability about the process, you're communicating how much you care about the overall experience your client receives. This display of empathy adds a tremendous amount of credibility to you. Not only do you want a client to feel good physically when the massage is over, you want her mental state to be just as relaxed and calm. A hundred massage therapists could perform practically identical full body massages, but a client will return to the therapist who goes beyond the muscles and orchestrates the entire experience to be handled with professional quality.

When we are explaining the process, we go so far as to use hand gestures to help describe what we mean. You might have noticed we use the word "underpants" in our spiel. "Underpants" is not a word we use in our everyday conversation. When we say "underpants," we put our hands at our waists to indicate the piece of clothing worn under one's pants. Prior to settling on this choice of words, in the past, when a client asked if they could leave on their "underwear," we realized in several different instances that underwear can mean different combinations of garments; bras, hosiery, camisoles, etc. So, if a female client gets confused about what the word *underwear* defines, sometimes using the word *underpants* seems to help clarify this. And I'm sure geographic location, educational level and religion only complicates this further – so find the words that simplify the process for you. Likewise, in describing what part of the chest or torso will be worked, we place our hands on our own chests to show how far we will go. We don't want a woman to feel like there could be the possibility of her breasts being touched. Similarly, a pre-massage explanation can often slam the door shut on any inappropriate ideas from clients to therapists. Your clients will come in with all sorts of misguided ideas, but when you are very particular in addressing all those common misunderstandings before the massage, you reduce the chances for embarrassment (on yours or the client's part,) impropriety, and the anxiety from a lack of understanding. For our practice, any request for specific glut work is always addressed through the sheet unless we receive voluntary consent to undrape the gluts. Likewise, abdominal work, as important as it to bodywork, is not apart of an initial session, unless requested and breast work is not approached without in depth discussion, documentation and signed consent.

The questions you ask about the needs of your clients must be framed with a true sincerity and a deep understanding and recognition of the meaning behind the words. When you attempt to perform a prescribed technique and "do the dance" without any modification, you will fail to meet the needs of many clients simply because a single set of movements will not be sufficient for everyone.

> *A massage session should never be about what the therapist wants to give. Rather, it should always be about what the client wants to receive.*

If you find out how someone wants to feel when she gets up, you will get all sorts of answers. Some clients tell us, "I just want to feel like…." Others say, "I want to feel worked over," or "I want to stop hurting." If we tried to do our "dance" of massage, there would be a good chance we would miss the mark. When the client can tell you how she wants to feel, it is your job to utilize your skills to create that desired effect. To the client, that is a good massage for that session. It may change the next time. A massage should never be about what the therapist wants to give. Rather, it should always be about what the client wants to receive. Private practice is very different from a spa setting. In a spa you can expect a fairly standard need from most clients. They want to relax and be pampered because often the spa environment dictates outcome, in all its various aspects. But when you are running a private practice, unless you ask, you literally have no idea why a person has come to you. If you always stop and find out what they want from each new session, you will be delivering the particular service they want each time. In doing so, each experience builds on the former to create a strong, long-lasting affiliation between you and the client.

When you ask questions and keep historical notes and files, you will be better able to attend to the current needs of the client for each individual session. Those notes provide the basis for a continuing relationship because each time a client comes in it is like starting from scratch. You can't assume, in most cases, that a client will want or need exactly the same massage every time. Some clients, of course, will not want you to deviate at all, but everyone's circumstances change from day to day. The first massage you give someone might be a result of a gift certificate that was used for a relaxation massage, but that same client six months later may have strained her muscles training for a marathon and need something completely different. Two months after that she may have been in a car accident and hurt her neck. More times than not, your clients' needs will change over time, but if you attempt to give your clients the massage you want to give, you will hamper your ability to retain them.

When the client comes in the next time (whether it's next month or next year,) we refer to the notes we've taken from the previous massage. We ask them questions like, "What did you like last time?" "Is there anything you'd like to change?" "Has your situation changed since your last massage?" If we assume because a client initially came in for relaxation, she wants the same thing, we put ourselves at risk of losing her. The changes may vary from requested levels of massage pressure, to less table heat to specific areas of concentration. If we don't remember what the last massage was like, then we have no way to make any alterations to the fixed or variable qualities of our practice. This is where the bottom half of the intake form comes into play.

Use SOAP Notes: To Help YOU Remember

We've mentioned before that most clients are not weekly visitors, and once you have a decent client base, there's no way you can recall each client's last massage. Consider a client returning to you after six months. If he were to tell you he liked his last massage but wanted you to work harder, how would you know the amount of pressure you used before? What if he told you his neck hurt? Where would you look to remember if his neck always hurt or has become a recent problem? The SOAP notes should give you that information instantly.

SOAP stands for "Subjective, Objective, Assessment, and Plan." We use them on every client, so we know what kind of service we've provided in the past and to continue recording the changes over time. The "Subjective" component occurs at the interview. We record what the client says about how she feels. "I'm stiff." "My back hurts from sitting in a bad office chair." "My feet are killing me." List descriptions for symptoms, locations, intensity, duration, and frequency. It is the information necessary to prepare in our minds what the client needs. The "Objective" component is the actual massage and any observations that are a result of any test you administered during the session. The "Assessment" component documents how the client was before the massage and how she is afterwards, any changes in the client as a result of treatment. "Neck muscles extremely tense and knotted before. Smooth and relaxed after." "Plan" may or may not be applicable. It may be in our minds or an actual plan to continue certain stretches or drink additional water. Remember that any actual direction or suggestions you give a client to use between massages should always be within your scope of practice. The last three components are recorded directly following the massage, so any therapist in our office working with this client can have access to the information the next time that client comes in.

When an existing client reschedules, we pull her file the day of her massage. When we conduct the pre-massage interview, we reference the last massage and her intake form for the current session. When she indicates a need for an increased concentration on her feet, we can see from her previous massages that this has not been an issue before. We can ask questions accordingly. When we know something new is going on, we can utilize the appropriate techniques to address that need. The same is true for pressure, based on our numbering system for pressure. If someone wants more or less pressure, then we know what she means.

SOAP notes can be used as a direct retention tool. It allows us to keep clients happy and give them what they need. If we know a client wants a head rush by working for twenty minutes exclusively on the head, it will be on file. We can ask at the pre-massage interview, "Did you like that head work last time?" Clients will appreciate the attention to their individual circumstances. Imagine the impact it has on a client you haven't seen in four months if the first thing out of your mouth is, "How is your neck feeling?" or "Have you have much lower back pain since I saw you last time?" People like to feel like they are known, that they are remembered that their symptoms and conditions are important to you. When you have detailed immediate notes about them they feel special. They won't care that you do the very same thing to every client because they will be impressed that you remembered them, especially those individuals you rarely see. When you treat each client like she is your most important client, it has a tremendous impact on how she perceives you. If each client believes this, why would they ever think of going somewhere else? Treating every client like a VIP, whether he comes in 52 times a year or once, is the simplest, and most cost-effective way to retain clients and get repeat business. You have them right there in your office at their own choosing. You haven't called and interrupted dinner or cluttered their e-mail inbox.

We're not suggesting you write a book on every client, and we're guilty of sometimes making rather vague notes, but we put enough information down to allow us to recognize what a client has already experienced in relation to what she needs now. Because there are multiple massage therapists in our office, and the SOAP notes stack up, there is some vital information about a client's ongoing needs that cannot be overlooked. We write those requirements on the outside of the folder, so there is no chance for them to be missed. The same is true if you are the only person giving your clients massages. Allergies, joint replacements, critical implants are some of the essential data we need listed. We have one client who is extremely allergic to tea tree oil. Because it is a constant need, it's on the outside, so whoever is giving the massage for that session will know without a doubt not to use it. We also have a client who has had double hip replacement surgery. If we did not have that critical information easily accessible, one of us might use compression without knowing, and that client would be quickly heading to the emergency room (and probably never back to us!) Both of these clients are sporadic, and in an effort to provide them with all they need, we protect ourselves from making a critical, costly mistake.

Create a Scale of Pressure

In addition to the description of the massage and any relevant consistent needs, we have developed a scale of pressure, as we indicated a couple of paragraphs back. We include this number on all clients, so in the event someone wants more or less pressure in a subsequent massage, we know exactly what we've done in the past. We recommend a scale from 1-10 with 10 being the highest degree of pressure. For us, 7 is standard pressure. You will have your own designation for what is your standard. It might be 5 or 6. Whatever you choose as your normal level of pressure, you can modify a client's massage needs based on it. If we do a massage at a hypothetical pressure level of 7 and the client requests a firmer massage, our SOAP notes tell us exactly what to do. If we hadn't made those notes from the last massage, "more pressure" would be arbitrary. Without knowing what level of pressure you've given in the past, your random application of "more" could be exactly the same as before, and the client will be disappointed. You may work on a hundred people before that client comes back to see you, but it is only her second massage. She's going to remember how much pressure you used the last time, and when you don't give her what she's asked for, her impression will be that you weren't listening and in turn, don't really care.

If you are just starting out your practice, you will have to develop your scale as you go, and if you've been in practice a while, you know the differences you personally use when it comes to pressure. Giving pressure a number increases your chances of giving a repeat client exactly what she needs each time. The scale of pressure and the SOAP notes are also extremely helpful when you see a client who normally goes to another therapist. There's no way you can know how the other therapist works beyond what the client tells you. If someone tells you she normally goes to a therapist who worked really deep but she'd prefer something lighter, you can decrease your pressure and then make a note of the pressure you used in relation to what the client said about the other therapist. Without the notes, you'd never be able to recreate that scenario on a return visit. If someone is searching for a new therapist or is new in town, your attentiveness to his previous experiences can make the differences between him staying with you or continuing his search.

After the Massage

When the massage is over, you are in your best position to present yourself and your services. Once the client resurfaces, we ask how they feel. You may be done with your hands-on part, but the massage session is not over. Remember, massage is bigger than the hour. The client is still returning to the world, and the way you interact from the moment they arrive to when they leave is your opportunity to extend the pleasurable experience. This time is critical for client retention. Once a client is dressed again and opens the door, the therapist is right back with the client. We offer some water and inquire about how they felt the massage went. We also explain that the next time they come in we will ask if there is anything they'd like differently. We plant the seed of returning without pressure. We want clients to understand they are directing their own massage and the frequency of their visits.

This post-massage time is just as much a routine for us as the pre-massage interview. First, we want to be sure they got what they needed and that the next time they can request changes. With our practice, we want them to know they can book with any therapist, and we explain pricing and our package pricing. Then, we discuss scheduling and rescheduling. By the time they leave, we want to have covered all this information. We do it at this time because it is still part of the experience. They are coming down from the physical part, so talking about what happens next is the best time to sell your self and your company. They are thinking about you and what you've just done for them. If you try to sell yourself outside the office a week later, you've missed your chance to have the biggest impact on your clients' minds. The relationship the client has asked for is only in your office. They have not invited you into their home life or to call them a week later. What they prefer you remember are the details of their wonderful massage.

When we finish a client's first massage with us, we go into more detail about modalities and future massages. For instance we explain we did a Swedish massage with a little trigger point, myofascial release, and myoskeletal alignment (or whatever combination of techniques was appropriate for that session,) so they understand that the various techniques we offer aren't a menu. It is more important to fulfill the requests based on how she wants to feel. Again, it's about UPR (unconditional positive regard), and being present. If a client has been to see us several times, we don't need to check in as thoroughly because we've established a relationship. We still want to know if needs were met and give the opportunity to articulate any alterations in the session or techniques desired or requested for the next appointment. The point is once the actual massage is over you still must have interaction with your clients to complete the full experience. If you recall how we schedule clients every 1½ hours for a one-hour massage, you can understand why it's important to allow the extra time between massages. We consciously choose to reduce our revenue in the short-term because we know how valuable the times before and after the massage are to bringing those clients back to see us.

Instead of $65 for an hour massage, we're giving them 1½ hours for the same price. We may not see nine clients in a day, but we're making far more in terms of giving our clients what they need from start to finish. If we chose to see nine clients a day and five of them didn't get what they needed, we would soon have to replace those five dis-satisfied clients with new ones. If we continued to fail to fulfill each client's need, we'd simply be treading water. Instead, we give technically more than a client has paid for because we're counting on that extra time to be our only chance to retain her. And, it doesn't cost us a penny out of our pockets. We don't have to create flyers or send e-mail or make phone calls because all our retention efforts are concentrated during the massage and the times before and after it. It's really the most valuable time you need, and it frees you up from spending your time chasing down uninterested clients.

Rescheduling Clients

When we try to reschedule clients, we leave the invitation open-ended and non-threatening. It has taken us some time to discover the best way to handle this direct opportunity to get repeat business, but through trial and error, we have come up with a method that fits our style. It also helps us to forecast revenue and project sales. We used to tell clients, "Just give us a call when you want another massage." That approach creates no urgency at all and offers no call to action. We adjusted how we handled this situation by changing it to a question. Without being aggressive or pushy, we ask, "Would you like to reschedule now, can we get you back on the calendar, or would you like to give us a call?" Presenting the future massage in this way offers a direct, though non-confrontational proposal. The client has two choices to pick from. She can make the appointment while she's in the office or wait until another convenient time.

By presenting your services in this fashion, you're basically asking, "Do you want to book your next massage right now or later over the phone?" Either way you are suggesting another massage and subliminally you are extending the present experience. You give the client complete control within a specific set of boundaries. There are two choices now. Easy choices left completely to the client. A higher percentage of sales are closed by asking than not. However, in marketing, the language used is a key and it doesn't matter if it is face-to-face like this scenario or with print strategies. That slight alteration from "give us a call" to "would you like to reschedule", can make a tremendous difference in the response you get. "Call us again sometime" is more like another way of saying goodbye and suggests you have already moved on to your next appointment. "Do you want to reschedule now or later?" presumes the client wants another massage, and all you're doing is offering two options on how to go about making that happen. By asking the "either/or" question, you eliminate awkwardness, and give your client options. If you're thinking, "I've got to get this person back as soon as possible," you're missing the bigger picture of what that client represents for you.

Be careful not to be too forward in rescheduling a client. If you have given her what she needed for that particular massage, she will consider you her massage therapist. There's no need to say, "Let's get you back on the books before you go." It's too invasive and aggressive, and that kind of language is diametrically opposed to the environment of the massage. Recognizing that the moments just after the massage has concluded are crucial to sustaining the entire experience means you must maintain the same demeanor of warmth and client-centeredness. You can give the most fantastic massage ever, but if you see your job ending upon completion of the hour, you leave your clients fending for themselves. Being bigger than the hour and finishing the experience is critical. Persuading someone to schedule another massage should be as warm and inviting as your touch.

In the end, clients will appreciate the overall experience and carry that with them from massage to massage. When you are present and spend that extra time with intention to strengthen the positive impression of you and your service, clients will gravitate to you. By fulfilling their massage needs each time and honoring their requests, however unusual they might be, it creates an unparalleled mental reaction. When you expand your reach beyond just the muscles to that place in their memories, in person and with genuine sincerity, you will consistently bring in more repeat business than any other traditional marketing strategies. Taking this long-term approach to retention gives you more time to be present for your clients. Everyone wants to feel special. As a business owner, this one-on-one time will make a larger impression on an already satisfied client and frees you from spending countless hours and dollars distracting your clients from the rest of their lives.

Chapter 10

Summary and Things to Consider

Principle 7: Massage is Bigger than the Hour

- Regardless of how often the client comes to see you - they always anticipate the massage.
- For the client, the massage BEGINS once they know the date and time of the next massage.
- Ask, how do you want to feel after the massage?
- Define your own "speech before undressing". This rehearsed speech will help you determine your effectiveness in communicating to the client what will take place during the session.
- SOAP notes are required by law, but can also help you to better attend to the needs of your client and their individual session.
- Create a scale of pressure to help define what you type of work you did with that particular client during that particular massage session.
- SOAP Notes stand for:
  - o Subjective: what the client says about how she feels
  - o Objective: the actual massage, scale of pressure and our
  - o observations during the session

o Assessment: documents the difference is how the client was before the session and how the client was after the session

o Plan: could be an actual plan of action for the client or plan for what to address in the next session.

Section IV

Creating a Sustainable, Referral Business

Creating a Sustainable Referral Business

Creating a sustainable referral business is often confused with word of mouth advertising. When we talk about referral business we mean someone is sending you business because you have initiated and developed a relationship of trust or because the person sending the referral looks good herself. To generate a referral source you must have a unique relationship with someone where you help build her business and she helps build yours. By our definition then, referral marketing has nothing whatsoever to do with your clients per se. It is all about business-to-business relationships.

When clients send others to you because you've done a good job for them, you are receiving a gift passively, we call that an accidental referral. You did good work on Uncle Lou. Uncle Lou tells Cousin Vinny and so on. You did nothing from a marketing standpoint to get that new business. Word of mouth or accidental referrals are naturally going to occur if you satisfy the needs of your existing clients and simply let it happen. Massage therapists like to believe they are doing referral business because one client sends one new person their way. This is a very limiting viewpoint of the power of referrals because you're expecting clients to work your business for you. Not all clients will even think about actively searching for new clients for you, and truthfully, it's not their responsibility to keep you in business. That is not to say when we get referrals from our clients we aren't grateful to them, but those individual referrals end up being small fish in a very big pond.

We're not interested in pursuing our clients for the names of people they know. Many clients are turned off by this kind of request anyway. They may thoroughly appreciate all you do for them, but they may be uncomfortable selling you to someone else. Selling yourself is part of being in business, and your clients aren't coming to you as other business people, though they very well may be in business. They are coming to you as massage clients with one goal in mind—massage. Pressuring them to send you clients is a huge turn-off. Consider this same situation at a restaurant. You wouldn't want your server to bring your bill after a fantastic meal and ask, "Can you call your friends to come and eat at my table?" It seems a little crazy in that situation, but massage therapists, believing they have a closer, more intimate relationship with clients, assume clients will want to help them beyond their own massages.

A lot of gimmicks are used to entice clients to send referrals such as promising to give discounts or free massages. The closest we come to suggesting this to clients is to offer a free massage for every five referrals, but it isn't something we push. When you try to manipulate or coerce your clients into giving referrals, you'll most likely be disappointed by the results. You want your clients to think of you when massage comes up in conversation; and they'll do more to convince their friends to come see you out of excitement, then to think about how irritated they are at being asked to send referrals. You cannot act out of desperation. This subtle shift from desperate measures to a passive confidence will increase your reputation, whether or not your clients ever mention a word about you.

Learning how to find referral sources from businesses is an extension of the principles for attracting clients from the first section. Massage therapists often dislike situations where they have to engage in "business" tactics, but developing relationships with others who can truly build your business is far more profitable in the long run than hoping all your clients send their friends and family to you. Finding those key business relationships might seem a little daunting, but in reality, you probably already have several relationships you are underutilizing as far as your business goes. The final two chapters explain a couple of ways to generate sustainable referral sources to increase your long-term business.

Chapter 11

Principle 8:

Massage Your Network

*"The greater danger for most of us
is not that our aim is too high and we miss it,
but that it is too low and we reach it."*

~ Michelangelo

Whether you are fresh out of school or you've been in practice for a while, there are people who are interested in your success. They may be friends, family members, or the acquaintance who works out beside you at the gym. A casual conversation about massage and what you do can open doors you were not even aware of, but you have to take the initiative to develop those relationships from a business standpoint. We don't mean every word out of your mouth should be about massage, but when you are looking for opportunities to build your practice, you are more attentive to the things people say. Refer back to Live your Business and creating your Introductory Speech.

Massage therapists often fail to see the impact these existing relationships can have because they concentrate their energy on convincing a single person to become a client. We've stated several times why attempting to get friends and family to be clients can cause serious damage to your practice, but fundamentally, those people do want to help you be successful. Their value to you is not in giving them a massage every once in a while and collecting a fee; it has everything to do with who they know and who they can introduce you to. Is your aunt a nurse in the neo-natal unit of the hospital? Is your cousin the office manager at a local company? Is your father the president of the neighborhood watch program? What does your workout partner do for a living? Expanding your practice through referrals has everything to do with networking the relationships that already exist around you. It's best to develop those relationships from the unique extended perspective of your massage therapy practice. If you spend your time trying to recruit everyone you already know to come to your table as a client, you're missing out on the greater potential they represent as referral sources.

When you shift your focus from trying to make your immediate circle of friends and family into clients, to utilizing friends and family for the people they know, you will begin to see how much more they can help you. Before they can give any assistance though, you have to know how they can best assist you. They want you to succeed, but then you have to go the extra step and explain what that success means and how they can help. (Refer back to the Introductory Speech.) You can't automatically assume that anyone understands exactly what you're trying to accomplish. Simply saying, "I want to have 30 clients a week" probably doesn't mean a lot to someone who has never run a business or knows very little about massage therapy. Where are those thirty clients coming from? Do you want to concentrate on sports massage or pain management or women or some other demographic? Who are the groups you want to be introduced to? Which companies would you like to get your foot in the door? Once you have defined those various groups, then you have something specific to ask for.

If you want to be known for pre-natal massage, you can ask your cousin, neighbor or your spouse's co-worker, "Who do you know who is pregnant?" or "Do you know anyone who teaches Lamaze or Hypno-Birthing classes?" Whatever you've chosen as your target groups, frame your responses to casual inquiries about your business with as much detail as possible. When you ask, "Know anyone who needs massage?" you'll probably get a lot of blank stares. How would anyone know that need about another person with any certainty? Your friends might know half a dozen people who **might** be interested in massage, but they probably aren't going to start a conversation with, "So, is your back stiff? I know a good massage therapist." But, when you are specific, and someone is genuinely interested in trying to send business your way, that individual will be much more able to recognize your potential clients. Oh, I see you're pregnant; I bet your back hurts, have you ever thought about getting massage while you're pregnant? I know a practice in town that specializes in pre-natal massage and I know the owners. By initially asking your question, you've given them the words to use, on your behalf. Instead of asking who needs massage, you might ask, "I know your son is involved in sports in high school, do you know any of the coaches?" Or, "I understand you play tennis, can you introduce me to the recreation director of your development?" You still only have a 50/50 chance your friend will have a relationship with who you are trying to attract as a client, but you narrow the field when you define your potential client.

What is at issue here is your predetermined description of your target market. You have to know what you are looking for before anyone ever asks. If you don't have a clear idea of the types of groups or businesses you'd like to be a part of you can't expect anyone to figure it out for you. When someone asks how she can help you, you have to be ready to answer that question without hesitation. Your immediate reply should be, "Who do you know who…?" When the answer is clear in your mind, explaining it to someone who cares whether you succeed or fail will see it clearly too. "Who do you know who coaches high school students, who do you know who is pregnant, how do you know who heads up the wellness committee at your company?" "Oh, you're looking for athletes. The high school soccer coach was my roommate in college. I could introduce you." It's really that simple, especially when you're talking to people you are already familiar with like friends and family. In many cases, your role as a massage therapist and business owner is nebulous and misunderstood by those people closest to you. They know you are a massage therapist and business owner, but they really don't know what that means or that their efforts can be invaluable to help you. You'd be surprised though what a little descriptive explanation can produce. It's like a light bulb going off in their heads.

When someone asks how they can help you, you have to be ready to answer that question without hesitation. Your immediate reply should be, "Who do you know who…..?
…works at a computer all day?
…is pregnant?
…drives long distances?
…was recently in a car accident?
…works in construction?
…trains for marathons or bodybuilding?
…holds a camera all day?
Who do you know who stands on their feet for a living?"

Friends and family can be a great resource for making some connections to groups you want to attract, but there is a limit to how much they can help you. The relationship you have with them was built outside the world of business, and no matter how much they might want to see you become wildly successful, you will always remain a relative or friend first. When you are looking for referrals in the business community, you have to be involved in the business community. You have to establish and develop relationships with business people who view you as a colleague and businessperson. There is a tendency, with service providers especially, to try and attach your self to a business without a personal relationship. Massage therapists like to think they have a referral source if they ask a business owner to display business cards and brochures near the cash register, but that doesn't mean that person is directing any of his customers your way. The business relationship must be there before you have any chance of getting referrals from someone. Plus, you'll get referrals faster if there is a benefit to the referral giver.

The quickest way to get your literature all over town is ask businesses to put it out for you. Unfortunately, this tactic is relatively useless compared to the amount of time and money it takes to make it happen. Without a relationship, there's no incentive. It's more like a favor. "Sure, you can put your business cards on my counter. What is it you do?" Those people aren't going to go out of their way to send anyone your way because you've simply shown up unannounced and begged for a small corner of a countertop. Massage therapists and small business owners mistake this willingness to display information as referral business - when this effort doesn't generate new clients anyway. This scenario is often the result of a misguided belief that certain kinds of businesses are more compatible with massage therapy and thus eager to refer their own clients. You have to keep in mind that if you thought it would be a good idea to ask the chiropractor to display your business cards, dozens of massage therapists before you thought the same thing. Trust and familiarity are the key factors in having someone send referrals, not a card on the edge of a counter. And, when those are non-existent because there is no business relationship, you can expect very little return on your investment.

If You Don't Have A Network, Build One

If referral business begins with a business relationship, then you have to have relationships with the right kinds of people. Once you have exhausted your existing circle, you have to move farther out. Massage therapists don't like to entertain the notion that the business community as a whole is their biggest asset. They see themselves in one-on-one conversations in a controlled environment, safely tucked away behind the door of their office. They are warm, inviting and work intimately with their clients. This scenario sounds nice and cozy, but the reality is if you see yourself building your practice to capacity and beyond, those warm and fuzzy, touchy-feely approaches aren't going to get you anywhere with business people you don't have business relationships with.

It may seem harsh and cold, but while our particular profession is personal and tactile, the business community does not function that way. You don't have to have a split personality when it comes to interacting with the larger world of business, but you do have to adjust your approach. Most businesses; massage or otherwise, have to establish business relationships in order to survive. Businesses tap into new potential by placing themselves where those opportunities exist. Advertising and direct marketing only go so far when it comes to generating new business, especially with massage. At first, people aren't going to just show up at your door; you have to go to them, and networking with businesses is one of the most profitable ways to reach people in masse who can benefit from your services—if it's done correctly.

There are only so many people with whom you have an existing relationship that can be developed into a business referral source. Eventually, you will have to extend your scope to create business relationships that don't exist yet. Practically every city in the country has networking opportunities freely available to local businesses. The local Chambers of Commerce, Merchants Association, or privately owned organizations such as Business Networking International (BNI,) or Action International, provide members with ways to make connections with other businesses. If you see these as cold and unfeeling, as many massage therapists do, you are missing out on the largest single source of direct contact with referral sources available. Many local Chambers of Commerce, or similar business organizations, offer members and guests monthly networking events or learning seminars to meet other businesses. These mixers are a critical component to building relationships that can lead to sustainable business for you.

A networking event is a chance for you to make connections to businesses, not individuals, with whom you may want to develop a stronger alliance. Unfortunately, many individuals approach these networking events as a chance to make an immediate sale. Networking is not about scheduling sessions or immediate sales, and because there are so many attendees with this mindset, massage therapists can get the impression that mixers go against the grain of everything they represent. They believe it is a group of strangers gathered together trying to collect business cards and sneak away with a slice of business. If done correctly, networking events might feel cold and impersonal, however; there's as much one-on-one interaction at a networking function as there is inside your office, but the environment, circumstances and the objectives are completely different.

In these settings you have to think of yourself as a business owner. You're a business owner who happens to operate a massage therapy practice. It's a minor mind shift with a major impact on the success of attendance. Your objective is to get as many people as possible to meet you and recognize you as a massage business; it is not your objective to schedule as many people as possible or to hand out as many business cards as you can. The mistake massage therapists make most often in talking with new people is imagining them as clients and presenting an assumed professional closeness. They approach complete strangers as if they are already a client. That assumed professional closeness, trust, and inviting demeanor that is completely necessary in a massage session cannot be effectively created in a networking environment. That doesn't mean you can't be yourself, but you have to avoid the temptation to cross uninvited boundaries as though this person were lying on your table. Imagine how you would feel if an accountant introduced himself to you and suggested at 1st meeting that it would be a good idea if you to let him look at your last three tax returns. You'd probably be instantly protective and slightly defensive and put off by such a forward, uninvited suggestion. When you network, you converse with people casually and naturally, but you do it with an intention on the long-term potential of building the business relationship.

In fact, don't even burden yourself with viewing the business opportunities with the individuals in attendance. Each person represents a company, a circle of contacts, even if he/she is just a one-employee business. When you talk to a sales rep for a local company, you have to see passed her to what she represents. If you spend all your efforts convincing her to get a massage, you miss the chance of developing a relationship where she could introduce you to the entire payroll of employees. Which is better—one massage or a personal introduction to the human resources manager of a 300-employee organization? It is somewhat unnatural, at first, to take this global approach when it comes to talking to an individual, but it isn't fake or misleading because the people who go to networking functions aren't in a buying mindset. They are busy networking. They aren't searching for products and services, so don't go with a selling agenda. Whatever you pitch in the way of direct sales will usually fall on deaf ears. Go with the intention to meet people who can help advance your business. To some this idea might sound cheap and inauthentic. Stop viewing the other networking people as potential clients and view them more as potential referral sources.

Networking is about meeting people. It requires an assumed assertiveness. It's about putting yourself in a location where other businesses are. There are so many business relationships you can establish by getting involved in this community, but you have to be willing to understand the role of a networker. A networker is someone who realizes business relationships come before the resulting business. A networking event then is solely about looking for the <u>right</u> relationships. Massage therapists judge the value of attending a mixer by whether or not they booked a client, and when they don't get immediate business, they assume these functions just aren't suited to massage therapy. When you go with the objective of getting your name out into the business community and creating recognition among the movers and shakers in town, you've gained a far more useful tool than the money you might receive from a single massage. Because many massage therapists tend to have such an aversion to networking, you will have very little competition and very little expense other than your time. Think about it. Most networking functions are monthly. That means you have twelve free chances to expose other businesses to who you are and what you do without any other therapists around.

Massage therapists tend to look at people who regularly go to mixers as being very different from themselves, but if you talk to the owner of a catering company or a maid service, you are likely talking with someone who struggles with exactly the same things you do—namely, how to grow your business and how to get your name out to the community and recognizable. You operate a private massage therapy practice in the same way other small business owners operate their own business. Again, it's not about the direct individuals you speak to. When you exchange business cards with someone, don't focus on his name; concentrate on what kind of business he represents. Consider all the people he knows, all the people behind him, so to speak. Does he work for a web design firm? What does that mean? Who are his clients, suppliers, his employees? Do most of the employees sit all day in front of computers? What companies does his company work for? View the people you meet as bigger than an individual. This global approach gives you the ability to see beyond what one person might pay you for services. You are there representing your small business and how it, not just you as a massage therapist, could benefit another company.

When you go to networking events as a representative of your company and start to view the individuals you meet as representatives of other businesses, you start to see the larger networking picture. When you talk to a real estate agent, you realize you are really speaking with someone who is part of a real estate agency who works with mortgage bankers, moving companies, home inspectors, contractors, etc. Establishing a relationship with Sir Realtor means you have a potential connection to everyone he does business with, and isn't that much more profitable over time than getting him to become a client? When you meet an accountant, you realize she represents dozens of other businesses around town that might benefit from massage. Hoping the people you meet at events will become clients is short-sighted because once they become clients, you have an ethical obligation to leave them alone. Once the real estate agent becomes a client, then in the treatment room, he is no longer available to you as a business referral source. He may send individuals your way, but then you're passively engaging in word of mouth, not business relationship referrals.

Massage therapists think it is better to show an individual, through an actual massage, how beneficial it is. Then they attempt to get into their company because the client knows them. This is reversing the roles. Once someone becomes a client, you are her therapist and must conduct yourself exclusively as her therapist, not a business associate. There are many clients we could manipulate to give us introductions into their companies, but we'd cross an ethical line if we did so. Initially, we would much rather keep the relationship on a business level to maximize the potential a person represents, rather than only make a few hundred dollars from her over the course of the year. You wear two hats as the owner of a private massage therapy practice. One hat is worn as the professional massage therapist behind closed doors working on clients. The second hat is as the owner of the business. At networking events, wear your business owner hat and capitalize on the vast opportunities there.

Business Cards and Their Role

Many business people, including those outside of massage therapy, believe the more their business cards are floating around a networking event the better. Consider the real impact of handing out business cards. If you go with the objective of giving your business card out to as many people as possible, remember that the people to whom you've handed your card have received fifty other business cards from others doing the same thing. The problem is now your card is co-mingled with those from the cell phone rep, the lawn service guy, the life insurance salesperson, and the staffing agency person. Your business name becomes diluted by all the other people that person met, and it doesn't really mean anything to him. A business card is nothing more than a piece of paper; it is not sufficient as a representation of your practice. The receiver of your card has no idea whether or not it is valuable to him, and if your brief conversation at the event was about the benefit of individual massage, he might not need or want massage himself and subsequently throw your card away. Whatever time you spent with him will have been a wasted opportunity.

You should always have business cards with you, but you should be more interested and focused in her card than yours. Her card represents her entire company, and it has all the contact information you need to follow up. A ten-minute conversation is never going to get you anywhere as far as referrals go, but when you send that person a note after the event and a flyer about your services and see her the following month at a networking function, you are multiplying the number of interactions and building a relationship that could develop into something beneficial to you. When you go to a mixer thinking about how many business cards you can collect, you're putting yourself in a much more powerful position. If you talk to twenty people and get their cards, you don't have twenty potential massages; you have twenty potential companies or organizations representing hundreds, even thousands, of massages.

Let's look again at the example of the realtor. An agent doesn't assume the people he talks to at a networking event need to buy or sell a house right then. His objective is to have as many people as possible recognize him as a real estate agent, so when the need does arise, his name is the first one to come to mind. Massage therapy is very much the same way. Most people you strike up a conversation with aren't going to need massage the next day, but they might in six months. Or, their company might be looking for someone to work a health fair, and if you are the primary massage therapist that's best known in the business community, who is going to get the call? You will because no other massage therapist has taken the initiative to keep putting their names in front of the people who have the power to contract your services. When you view networking as the beginning of recognition, you can get beyond the need to walk around with your appointment book open, asking, "Who wants massage?" or "Would you like to come in tomorrow for a massage?" like the cell phone guy, constantly calling and asking to compare dollars on your service contract.

When we started attending networking events, we had no clue what to do to make it worthwhile. Unfortunately, we did nothing initially but stand in the corner talking to each other. We had technically attended, but we didn't achieve anything at all. If the thought of these events makes you uncomfortable because they seem so different from your normal mode of operation, you're not alone. Almost everyone there is counting down the time until it's over. We realized if it was going to benefit us at all, we had to shift our mindset and intention and be more assertive in our approach. Think of networking like you think of having a party at your house. Pretend you've invited 200 of your closest friends, neighbors and colleagues over to your house for a couple of hours. Think about how you would you act then? You'd probably walk around making sure everyone was enjoying them selves. You'd try to talk to as many of your guests as possible. You wouldn't feel out of place or uncomfortable. You'd greet them with warmth and enthusiasm, even if you couldn't remember their name. When you can own a networking event as if you yourself had invited the attendees, your focus completely shifts away from targeting them as clients to ensuring they are having fun. You take the time to get to know them, recalling what they do, inquiring where they live or the hobbies they invest their time in. Without the pressure to generate business immediately from an event, you can free yourself to meet people and concentrate on establishing fun, common connections with other business people for future development down the road.

Networking Groups

In addition to networking events held after hours, most places offer opportunities for you to be involved with a group of business people who meet regularly to help each other grow. Many of these groups are industry-exclusive, which means, in your case, you aren't competing with other massage therapists for the same relationships. A networking group is vital to developing long-term business relationships with people who share a common interest in business growth. The monthly mixers are great for meeting people you might not come in contact with anywhere else, but a group that meets regularly gives you a much more concentrated chance of building strong business relationships with people who are getting to know you. It's difficult to gain enough trust and credibility in a two-hour event, but when you see the same people week after week and work to understand each other's business needs, you have a greater potential for success.

Networking groups, like the mixers, are not about the members of the group becoming clients. It's always about who those group members know. If you invest the time to make real connections with the other members, they will be attentive to helping your business grow. It does take work though. Some people who join groups like this expect to start receiving referrals instantly just because of the membership. It doesn't work that way. Like any other relationship, you first have to find common ground, build a foundation and continue working on it. Since your objective is not to convince that member to get massage from you, you can focus on the business part of your practice. How can your relationship with the wedding planner help your practice? Consider bridal parties, honeymoon packages, etc. Does the financial planner work for a large firm? Give thought to their clients, tax time crunch, incentives. Who do the members know that you'd like to know? It is an active process, in which you must determine your goals and explain it clearly enough to others that they can help you reach those goals. The most seemingly incompatible businesses to massage therapy can have huge potential because of the relationships you develop. It doesn't matter that traditionally landscaping and massage aren't usually used in the same sentence. If you know the owner of the landscaping company, you can creatively find ways to make that relationship work to your advantage and for his. Who are his clients? What does he give his corporate clients for the holidays? How does he say thank you for your business? Maybe he'd be willing to say thank you with a free massage?

Massage Therapy, as with many other service industry groups, are financially supported by billable hours. Meaning: you work, you get paid and if you don't work, you don't get paid. So as a result, most people in service businesses see networking groups as time away from their money-making time. They think they can't afford to go to lunch for two hours and not book paying clients because they see it as lost revenue. It's not productive to view networking as separate from your business. The time you spend at a networking group is as vital to your practice as the actual clients lying on your table. Those couple of hours you spend networking can have a significantly greater impact on your success than the fees you collect from a couple of massages. A couple of sessions come and go, but the relationships you establish with other business people are far more stable and long-lasting, with the potential to generate endless referrals.

If you live in a relatively midsized city, you can probably find several networking groups already in existence. Invest the time to visit a few of them to see where you might fit in best. Even if you don't ultimately join one group, you will have networked anyway. The people you meet still have the potential to become referral sources for you if you make the effort to follow up. When you find a group you are comfortable with, get to know the members as business people. Wear your business hat and approach them with what they represent always on your mind. Our experiences with networking, both at after-hours events and in membership groups, have opened more doors for our practice than we would have ever seen had we waited by the phone for people to call. We continue to network because we know we might meet someone who knows someone else we want to know. Discovering a potential referral source can literally happen anywhere, as long as you have the right mindset, live your business, be present and think like a business owner. Since you never know who other people know, all your networking efforts eventually pay big dividends in one form or another. When you can look beyond the immediate dollar figure and/or the number of bodies on a table; those bigger rewards take the form of recognition, credibility, exposure, and trust. In the end it is these values, which are always with you, that give other business people a reason to refer your business in the first place. So get out there and network. Introduce yourself and your business with other business owners. Open the doors that other massage therapy business owners are afraid or unwilling to open.

Chapter 11

Summary and Things to Consider

Principle 8: Massage Your Network

- Shift your focus from making your family and friends into clients - into asking your family and friends to introduce you to the people they know.
- When you create business relationships - you create referrals.
- When you have exhausted your existing circle - look at the secondary circles. The woman you attend BNI with, also attends church, The Red Hat Society, is a member of the Rotary Club and volunteers at the Public Library. She is in your existing circle. All of her other memberships are secondary circles for you to pursue.
- View the person at the networking event as a representative of a company that employs over 500 employees. Look at those employees as the people you want to gain from networking event, not just the single person in attendance.
- Always, always, always carry business cards. When you get business cards at events, write something memorable about that person on the back of the card, maybe the

date, the location you met them, and the person who introduced you.

- Networking becomes easy when you change your mindset to look at the event as your party. You are the host, they are your guests.

- Who do you know who?

Chapter 12

Principle 9:

Build Win-Win-Win Relationships

"Adults invented work so they could keep playing together."

~ Silver Rose

Establishing and developing relationships with other business people can make an enormous difference in your massage therapy practice. But, those relationships have to be ones in which all parties involved benefit in some way. With most new businesses, it is a common mentality for referral business to result in the Win-Win scenario. Someone gives a referral, the massage therapist makes money (win;) and the client gets a massage (win.) Everybody wins, except the referral giver. The distribution of "winning" isn't equal, and it ends with the payment for services. It's really only one transaction. Getting referrals from others under these circumstances are limited to singular points in time and are more like recommendations than referrals. You, as the recipient of the referral, have not particularly utilized or developed any existing relationship but rather you've let someone come to you on the recommendation of someone else. This results in a waiting game you really can't afford to play. The clients will only trickle in. Expecting lucrative referral opportunities from this method is as ill-advised as assuming your phone number and business card will magically compel people to call for massage. All three parties must receive a benefit to create a Win-Win-Win, and this creates an active role for the Massage Therapist, Business Owner in building business relationships.

As we said in the last chapter, finding ways to network with other businesses in your community is the key to getting your name out to others with whom you can start relationships, but something has to be done with those relationships once the initial introductions have been made. Even before you ever attend a networking function, how can you capitalize on relationships you already have with other business people? Many business people in all kinds of professions think a referral source should consist of that person sending them new business, and massage therapists are no different. In order for the referral source to be successful, there must be a tangible and quantitative result, right? If not, then what's the point? Unfortunately, this viewpoint is very short-sighted and marginalizes the value of what relationships should be about in the first place.

> *The beauty of Win-Win-Win relationships is that the intangible, long-term rewards far exceed anything you might expect to gain immediately.*

In a Win-Win-Win situation, your objective should be to bring together two people plus yourself to form a triangle where all three parties gain something. The beauty of Win-Win-Win relationships is the intangible, long-term rewards far exceed anything you might expect to gain immediately. Why would you go to the trouble of connecting two other people so they can do business together? Because it makes you look good and it adds to your reputation (win,) and the two people who you have connected will appreciate you for having brought them together (win-win.) You are making an investment in the future of that existing relationship because when you give without expecting anything in return, you will be rewarded in unimaginable ways.

Sadly, there is a common scenario massage therapists run into all the time that perpetuates the misunderstanding about relationships and the importance of Win-Win-Win opportunities. It occurs right from the beginning for many therapists. As a therapist, you have to find or have a place to conduct your business and offer your services, and many people turn to places like spas, franchises or other similar locations, where they can work on clients on a limited basis. Typically the spa owner readily accepts your inquiry to include you on a list of massage therapists he can call in to do a massage for one his clients. As a subcontractor, they will require at least a 50/50 split (or more in some cases) of the money you generate. It feels unfair, but consider their business expenses; their building rent, mortgage or lease, their company name and reputation, they've paid for the advertising, they furnish the room, equipment and supplies, and they've cultivated the clients. It's fair that they receive the residual revenue that comes from a steady stream of clients. But it doesn't allow independent massage therapists to build a client base on which to financially and independently support themselves. If your intention is to be a business owner, you will be better off, in the long run to begin the long road of self sacrifice right now rather than later. Leaving any business as a former employee or subcontractor will still basically result in starting from scratch to build your business. Beginning a business at any time during the life of a career will require that you reduce your initial income in order to build something for the future. What you will have gained in the long run, however; as an employee or subcontractor, that might save you time and money is 'experience'. The experience you might acquire would require you to be actively involved with the business owner watching them conduct business, plan, be flexible and strategize business growth and ask questions all along the way. Unfortunately, it's highly unlikely that many business owners would entrust a subcontractor with that level of information.

As a massage therapist, we encourage you to be careful of the spa owner or massage practice that pays only commission. As the therapist, you're taking the risk, not the owner. You'll need to plan for unpaid sick leave, unpaid vacation, and constantly varying paychecks. If you are supplementing your income and find yourself an opportunity like this, you will probably view it as a win-win-win situation. It's a viable solution, and financially the 50/50 split is smart on the behalf of the business owner, however if you're hoping to build your private practice in this way, you will come out on the short end of the stick and it will take you considerably longer to build a practice in the long run. The spa owner looks good to her clients, but the therapist leaves empty-handed—little money, zero clients. It's like renting an apartment. You have a roof over your head, but as soon as you decide to move elsewhere, you have nothing.

Starting a new business now or later will still require you to cultivate your own business relationships. And there are businesses and business opportunities available to you if you really look for them. Our philosophy, on the other hand, attempts to offer every massage therapist, either as a business owner or an employee, a piece of the reward over the life of the relationship.

For the business owner, we have flex space available, and we charge very little to the independent massage therapist who wants to utilize it. We *win* by making a small amount of money, but the massage therapist *wins* by having a cost-effective place to conduct massage, and the client *wins* by getting a great massage in a professional environment. The revenue we make from an individual massage therapist isn't our objective. Our reward is more intangible. If another massage therapist asks her about a suitable location to get started, who is that initial therapist immediately going to suggest? Because we don't try to squeeze every penny we can from individuals attempting to build their practices, our flex space is consistently used, and we also have a large list of massage therapists we can call on when we need them. The massage therapists also get an intangible benefit in that by not having to give back all their profits or invest in overhead they can't yet afford, they make more money, which allows them to continue practicing and growing their businesses. Another massage therapist's success is not a threat to us because the more successful massage therapists are the more widely known massage therapy is to the entire community. There's absolutely no way we can measure the impact greater exposure to massage therapy across the board will be for our practice, but we know we will ultimately win as a result.

> *Don't view another massage therapist's success as a threat. The more massage therapists are successful the more widely known massage therapy is to the entire community. That is a Win-Win-Win.*

If you decide to rent flex space or fulltime space, we encourage you to get the terms of the lease in writing. Protect yourself, protect your clients and protect your landlord.

Another way we conduct win-win-win business, now that our business has grown, is to offer licensed massage therapists a full or part time salaried position, including benefits, for those that don't have any desire to own a business. We provide everything; fully furnished treatment rooms, marketing and advertising, linens and supplies, receptionist, full service scheduling, a base salary with commission based earnings and opportunity for bonus pay, vacation and sick leave, and we most of all, we give the therapist an opportunity to work in massage therapy as a professional career without having to own a business. We find this to be the better solution than the "spa-subcontractor mentality". Employing salaried massage therapists means we take the risk up front, ensuring enough clients to fill their schedules and "pay for their positions", but in turn this provides an instant *win* to the therapist. A salary allows them the stability with which they can fully plan and finance their private lives; including vacations, personal interests, car loans, children and mortgages, without having to go through years of business growth and financial risk. Employing the therapist gives an instant *win* to the massage therapy practice. We have instant coverage, allowing us to know when we can schedule the clients and fill the schedule. Having employed therapists offers an instant *win* to the client, they receive consistency in their therapy and develop trusting relationships with the therapist and practice.

If you're an owner of a private practice in massage that employs therapists, we encourage you to be careful of the massage therapist that jumps on board for the salary, takes advantage of the steady income but leaves the company before they've hit their stride in meeting the weekly massage quotas. As the owner you're taking the risk, not the massage therapist.

In general, taking advantage of others is not a good idea, but people do it all the time without hesitation or conscious. Mostly, their actions result in taking advantage of people because they don't have the ability to see beyond the immediate situation. When you create Win-Win-Win relationships, you're beginning to create something good for everyone.

Make Your Own Relationships Work For You

Everybody knows people who work in other businesses. You do business with them yourself every day. You did business with them before you ever became a massage therapist. So who are those people in your life? Do you regularly buy flowers from the florist down the street? Is your next door neighbor in the carpet cleaning business? Does your local sporting goods store manager know you by name because everyone in your family participates in athletics, and you're always buying new gear? You know people in all kinds of occupations, but developing a Win-Win-Win relationship with them is not about the particular professions and how your service and their service can equally benefit the consumer. When you think about it this way, your focus is on your immediate reward. The short-sighted thinking goes something like this. "If I can get this business to hook up with me, then I'll get new clients because that person's clients need massage too." It's the fallacy that complimentary businesses are waiting for you to contact them. Using a relationship for your gain is much like the spa owner who sees the dollar signs in allowing massage therapists to pay him to work.

When you shift your focus away from your immediate benefit, you begin to look at the relationship in terms of how you can add value for that person and his clients. You can't be afraid of losing something because you've put two people together. Establishing connections so others can do business with each other isn't ever a loss for you. It isn't revenue in your pocket, but when you've fulfilled a need for another business person and a client to win, who are both of those people going to want to thank? YOU. Who are they going to think of when it comes to massage? YOU. When you bring other people together who can help fulfill their needs, you will always gain from the interaction over time.

A Win-Win-Win can happen between massage therapists and a client as well. A therapist who rents an office at our center came over to help us out with a client we could not see. She did the massage in our office, under our name, but she and the client made a real connection. The client had been to see us five times already, but we realized these two people had truly clicked. They had mutual interests and acquaintances outside massage. When the client was leaving, we handed her the other therapist's business card and told her she could contact her directly if she felt so inclined. Essentially, we were taking ourselves out of the picture, but we didn't lose in that situation. We didn't view it as losing because the other therapist gained. We saw it as a Win-Win-Win.

> *When you're able to bring people together who can help to fulfill eachother's needs, you will gain from the interaction over time.*

The therapist got a new client; the client got a therapist she really bonded with, and we received the priceless reward of knowing we made it happen. Our win was in knowing the massage therapist would continue to keep her office at our center, and if we needed assistance again, she would be willing to help us out. We were also able to show our client our unwavering dedication to seeing her needs met. Taking this long-range approach, especially when it comes to relationships you have with other therapists, propels your reputation in everyone's minds. When it comes to creating Win-Win-Win relationships with other therapists, you might find it hard to imagine how you could benefit, but if you see it as strengthening the bond you have with that therapist, you have a colleague you can count on and who might one day assist you in a large project you can't handle by yourself.

The same philosophy is true of your other relationships beyond the massage industry. Those existing relationships represent business opportunities if you will only be attentive to them. The philosophy of unconditional positive regard plays a role in how you see these relationships. When you genuinely want to make other people successful or benefit, they will naturally be drawn to you. By creating Win-Win-Win relationships without concentrating on what you will get or how much you will win, those individuals who benefit in tangible ways from your willingness to make it happen will want to repay you. Again, that repayment might not be in the form of a new client for you, but you want to be the first person they think of when a massage therapist is required. Someone might be looking for a speaker at a community group or health fair participant or gift certificate provider.

You just never know what kind of reward or call to action you will receive or when that reward may come. If you continue to foster the business relationships with an authentic desire to see everyone come out ahead, opportunities will come to you.

Say for instance, one of your clients has children, and each time she sees you she talks about the difficulty in finding good childcare. One of the people you have a business relationship with is a full-time nanny. You tell your client you know someone who could probably help her. When you put the two together, you have made no money, but you look good to both your client and the nanny. The nanny wins by getting a new client; your client wins by securing a reliable, trustworthy childcare provider. You have done something beneficial for the nanny and your client, and what you gain in the short-term is an increased sense of loyalty from your massage client. In the long run though, you have strengthened the relationship with the nanny. From that initial connection, you might suggest to the nanny to give out your discount coupons to her regular clients. When she does, she looks good to her clients; you might possibly get a new client, and the individual gets a quality massage. Everybody wins. And, when you create that initial Win-Win-Win with the nanny, the relationship grows and deepens and provides further foundation for more referrals.

> *If you continue to foster the business relationships with an authentic desire to see everyone come out ahead, opportunities will come to you.*

"Have a Cup of Coffee on Us"—A Win-Win-Win Example

On the ground floor of our building is a coffee shop. We established a relationship with the owner initially through our own patronage. That relationship naturally grew because of our close proximity and frequency of visits. We decided there was a way our practice and the coffee shop could work together to build each other's businesses. We suggested to the coffee shop owner we hand out free coffee coupons to our massage clients to go downstairs and have a free cup of coffee on us. Upon redemption of the coupon, we would pay the coffee shop one dollar per coupon. We stamped the back of the coupons with our logo, so the coffee shop owner would know the patrons were coming as a direct result of us sending them down. The coffee shop got new clients, and our clients got a free gift, which made us look good.

We received no money from sending our clients downstairs for a cup of coffee, but offered a small gesture of appreciation to them for getting massage, and we exposed them to the coffee shop. The coffee shop owner had the opportunity to showcase his products and store atmosphere to someone who might never have thought to stop there. In return for the business we send him, he displays our literature on his counter, and when he hears someone talking about massage, he only mentions our name. That's an intangible win for us because we have no idea who he may talk to about us, and we also don't know when or if an individual will book a massage based on that conversation. What we do know is because everybody wins in this relationship, good things will happen eventually. In a Win-Win-Win relationship, you have to accept "later" and "eventually" as smart business decisions.

If we had arbitrarily walked into the coffee shop and asked the owner to put our business cards on his counter, he might have said yes, but he wouldn't have gained anything from it. When you attempt to do this sort of short-cut thing with businesses who you don't have a relationship with, you are basically begging for them to market your practice for you silently. It never works to your advantage, and you will have wasted your time. When you ask yourself, "How can I make a business person I know more successful?" you are showing a care and concern for another's well being that's unmistakable. You set yourself apart from others in the business community who are spinning their wheels asking themselves, "How can I make myself more successful tomorrow?" Replace the "I need more clients soon" mentality with "I'm in this for the long haul; I'm 'all-in,'" so how can my services help another business look good to their clients? When you stop worrying about the immediate results of building relationships, you will begin to see the limitless possibilities of Win-Win-Win.

In this situation, it cost us nothing to hand out these cards. The client appreciated the gesture, and she could choose whether or not to accept it. If a client didn't want the coffee, we didn't waste our marketing dollars. In contrast, if you send a client a flyer in the mail, you have the costs of paper, envelope, and postage, plus your time, which together roughly equals a dollar. The difference is you don't know how well the mailing was received; you're not doing anything to benefit anyone but yourself. So, for less than the same price as an unwanted direct mail piece, we know from the number of cards redeemed, exactly what our clients' reactions are, and we're helping out another business. The flyer in the mail is most likely not going to bring a significant return, but this Win-Win-Win presents potential we cannot even begin to imagine.

> *One time we suggested to a coffee shop owner we could hand out free coffee coupons to our massage clients to receive a free cup of coffee. We stamped the back of the coupons with our logo, so the coffee shop owner would know the patrons were coming as a direct result of our business. Upon redemption of the coupon, we paid the coffee shop one dollar per coupon. The coffee shop got new clients and our clients got a free gift. So, for less than the same price as an unwanted direct mail piece, we knew from the number of cards redeemed, exactly what our clients' reactions were, and in return we helped another business. Another Win-Win-Win*

A Window Shopping Experience - A Win-Win-Win Example

There is a stationery store a couple of blocks from our office. The products the owner sells and her clientele have nothing whatsoever to do with massage therapy, but we have an existing relationship with her. We purchase things from her, and she's a massage client with us. We could leave it at that and be happy in the symbiotic Win-Win environment, but we walk into her store thinking about how we can utilize that relationship to create a Win-Win-Win. She offers engraving and screen printing on promotional pieces like bags, pens, etc. and displays them in her shop to let prospective clients know she sells more than cards and gifts.

We suggested to her that we would pay for the printing and embroidery if she would showcase those items in her window. She wins because she has a paid sample of her work to show potential customers. Her clients win because she can duplicate that quality for them, and we win because our name is prominently displayed in the window. By our paying for the product, she had no out-of-pocket expense, and that's another element of the win for her. We didn't ask her to refer her clients to us directly, but if someone comes in to order something similar to what is displayed, a conversation about us may start between them. The client may only be vaguely familiar with our practice, but seeing our name in this setting is another way for us to gain exposure, and it's significantly cheaper than a billboard. That person might tell the owner she's heard of us, and the owner will say positive things about our practice. Our objective was not to see the immediate results from paying for the engraving. We made the suggestion to make the stationery store owner look good. We knew doing so would be beneficial to us in the long run. She doesn't talk about any other massage therapists in town, and that's a win for us, even though if doesn't necessarily mean a client leaves her store and comes directly to our office to schedule a massage.

Win-Win-Wins are interconnected as well. The client who buys engraving from the stationery store might be the owner of another business. The stationery store owner, through her own relationship with her customer, might discover he is looking for employee gifts and suggest massage. When she puts us together with the business owner, we have an opportunity to create a new Win-Win-Win between us, the business owner, and his employees. In this case, we receive the tangible reward of selling gift certificates and gaining new clients. The business owner looks good to his employees, and the employees get massage. Plus, the stationery store owner elevates her own position in both our eyes and those of the business owner, so she receives the intangible reward. She's made no money by sending him to us, but she's made an investment in the relationship she has with us and the other business owner.

Who will that business owner come back to for future engraving? And then, who will he come to for massage? It might be six months or a year away, but when you are in business as a career, presumably for many, many years, six months is a short time. Furthermore, an employee who gets a free massage from his boss may want us to provide our services to his adult summer league softball team as a reward for winning the championship. We just don't know where our relationships will take us. It was a scenario similar to this one that we ultimately traveled to Greece. Not every relationship will lead to a display of unimaginable success, but then again we never expected the relationships we established and invested in several years ago would take us halfway around the world.

Make Your Own Top Ten List

There's no possible way we can tell anyone exactly where to find Win-Win-Win relationships. Only you know who you know, so make a list of ten people with whom you have an existing relationship. Don't think about their professions as an indicator of potential. Let the relationship guide the process. Think about how you can make that relationship benefit the most people, regardless of whether or not you get clients immediately or directly. It's infinitely easier to think about who you know than it is to figure out who can refer business to you. When you consider business people you already know, you are at a distinct advantage compared to anyone else attempting to start a relationship with that person. Who are they going to be more likely to respond favorably to—you or a stranger off the street?

Once you have your list, don't attempt to sell them massage. Figure out what your services can do to make them look good. You have to remember your goal is not to get the individual on your table because that's a minute source of income. For instance, if you know a relocation real estate agent because your children play basketball together, how would massage make her look good to her clients? Wouldn't her clients, who have just moved in from out of town, really appreciate a relaxing massage after a stressful transition? What better housewarming present is there? If you suggest to the agent that you will provide her free coupons, or discounted coupons, to give as gifts, the agent wins because she has given a memorable present. The client wins with a free massage, and you win by getting a new client who has probably not found a regular therapist. Perhaps you didn't make any money from that situation, but when the homeowner calls the agent to thank her for the fantastic gift, what's that agent going to do with the next house she sells?

> *Make a list of ten people with whom you have an existing relationship.*
> - *Don't think about their professions as an indicator of potential. Let the relationship guide the process.*
> - *Think about how you can make that relationship benefit the most people, regardless of whether or not you get clients immediately or directly.*
> - *Don't attempt to sell them massage. Figure out what your services can do to make them look good.*
> - *Be creative. Be willing to give something for nothing. Be willing to help someone else out.*
> - *Double check your process. Track your progress. Track the number of people you come in contact with. Document what you can do the next time that will improve the return on investment for everyone involved.*

By giving free massage coupons to the real estate agent, you're allowing her a cost-free way to increase her reputation with her clients. When people look good because of something you've done for them, the degree of appreciation and strength of that relationship builds your business. For all you know, one of those new people to your area may be a business owner too. In the future, he may be a referral source for you, and you might just create a Win-Win-Win relationship with him to help build his business. When you aren't clamoring for a sale, you look at the potential for you to win and another person to win. Then, it's all a matter of figuring out where that third win will come from.

When you build a relationship with people you already know and create a Win-Win-Win, both of those people you put together know people you don't know. Because of your efforts though, through a series of triangular relationships, you'll receive the tangible rewards because this person knows that person who knows somebody else. In the end, you are in the center of a huge matrix of interconnected relationships, all with ties back to you in one way or another—some of which have yet to be connected. But they will. When you are the person who makes things happen for others, more people know you. As you build your network of relationships, you will have so much more than a massage practice. You'll be a resource hub that other business people will want to tap into and be a part of, and it literally all starts with honestly finding out how you can make someone else's business grow.

> As you build your network of relationships, you'll find you are in the center of a huge matrix of interconnected relationships, a resource hub, all with ties back to you in one way or another.

If you can see beyond the first relationship layer to where it leads, you stop being overly concerned about what a single individual can do for you. We'll give one more example of the power of this principle. A massage therapist has an existing relationship with a jewelry store owner. She goes to him and says, "Why don't you give these free massages away to your best clients?" It cost the jeweler nothing, and he can thank his loyal clients with something more memorable than a thank you card. In the process, he looks good to his clients; those clients get free massage, and the therapist gets the potential to retain those people.

The people who are clients of the jeweler all have relationships with others around town, but because the therapist has done good things for both the jeweler and his client, she will stand out in both their minds. So, say the president of a local company buys a diamond necklace for his wife and receives the free massage. He gives it to his wife with the necklace, and she comes to the therapist's office for the session. The wife makes a strong connection with the therapist because the therapist gave her what she needed (unconditional positive regard) and tells her husband what a great experience it was. The wife becomes a regular client, but six months later the husband, who the massage therapist has never met before, comes on his wife's recommendation, to buy gift certificates for his employees. In the process of establishing this new relationship, she finds out he is the event director for a local charity organization that is planning a health fair in three months with an anticipated attendance of 1000 people. He wants the therapist to come and represent massage therapy. The therapist agrees and goes. At the health fair, the president introduces her to the human resources manager of a company he does business with. That manager has been searching fruitlessly for a good, reliable massage therapist to handle some high-profile executives who come to town every quarter. The therapist agrees (because she never says no,) and after the first quarter, the HR manager is thrilled at the service and wants the general sales manager to meet her to create an incentive and gift program for all the sales reps and their clients.

On and on it goes, but it started because you had a relationship with a jewelry store owner and found a way to make him look good to his clients. That scenario was the result of a single line of relationships and introductions. How many free massages will the jeweler give out? Probably as many as you give him, but why would he stop making himself look good? Consider if you gave him twenty free massages to give to special clients, and each one took a path similar to the one mentioned above. You wouldn't ever have to ask businesses to place your cards on their counters. As long as the jeweler continues to look good to his clients, they will be more likely to keep coming to his store, so his business grows, and he's a winner. The free massages you do as a result of him handing out your coupons builds your business, so as you develop and strengthen that relationship, you have a true Win-Win-Win referral source. You have to keep in mind this example spanned almost a full year, but the eventual rewards are well worth the wait.

If you can generate this kind of situation with a single business owner (and you can,) you can recreate it with all your existing relationships—if you can find out how everyone can win. It does take some creativity on your part and a willingness to postpone your tangible reward until a later time, but when you are marketing your business by attracting new clients and properly retaining existing ones, you can afford to wait for a Win-Win-Win relationship to come full circle. It can be difficult to be patient, but when you finally see what amazing things can happen as a result of your efforts, you won't be hesitant any longer about developing business relationships where everyone comes out a winner.

Chapter 12

Summary and Things to Consider

Principle 9: Build Win-Win-Win Relationships

- Win-Win-Win = Define what each party needs to achieve and what each party has to give - in order for each party to achieve a level of satisfaction.
- Make your own Top Ten List. People with whom you have existing business relationships.
  - o Coffee Shop Owner
  - o Hair Stylist
  - o Doctor
  - o Dentist
  - o School Teacher, PTA president,
  - o Real Estate Agent
  - o Coach
  - o Pastor
  - o Jewelry Store Owner
  - o Tanning Salon Owner
- What can you offer each of these people that will make them look good to their clients, add value to their clients lives, and in the end, make you look good?

Epilogue

Where Do You Go From Here?

"If you can't make up your mind decisively,
then you'll never learn to make money anyway.
Opportunities come and go. Being able to know when to
make a quick decision is an important skill."

"The moment you see one opportunity,
you will see them the rest of your life."

~ Robert T. Kiyosaki

Depending on where you are in your practice, you may be looking at a multitude of directions in which to go. Regardless of what your goals are for your practice, ultimately you do have to have clients to support your business, and these nine principles will help you build that client base to the level where you can sustain a thriving full-time practice. In the course of writing this book, we sometimes worried people might think, "Well, it's easy for you to say these things now. You're established. You don't have my same worries and concerns." It does become easier for an established, thriving practice to be patient and wait for profitable circumstances to come to fruition, but we started our practice just like everyone else. There's a saying in the poker world that applies to all new businesses—"All you need is a chip and a chair." You have to have the resources to play, and you've got to have a table to sit down to. Other than that, you are on an equal playing field, and it's all a matter of how you use what you start with. There will always be a massage therapist who has been at the table longer, but if you accept the fact that you have just as much opportunity as anyone else, you'll realize the tremendous potential uniquely in front of you and your private practice.

Some people are obviously going to fold their hands because they made misguided bets, but the true professionals know what is required of them to take the chip lead and win the prize. We made the decision to become successful business owners in private practice as massage therapists and we went "all-in." We put all our chips in the middle of the table. We were willing to put in all the time and effort, regardless of our comfort level, to become successful. As we mentioned before, the first month we had paying clients there were three of them. That was the January of our first year in business. Over the course of that year, we performed 470 massages between the two of us. It was in that year that we discovered and implemented many of the principles we've outlined here. We worked forty-hour weeks, regardless of client appointments. We never said no to a request for massage. We practiced unconditional positive regard with every single client who came to see us. We gave massage away, and we found groups and developed strong, lasting relationships with them. The following year we did over four times as many massages—1829 to be exact.

We don't live in an enormous city with a million people, and there are certainly plenty of other massage therapists in the immediate surrounding area. (We have access to over 80 massage therapists we can call on if we need them.) We simply stuck to our objectives to be both caring, devoted massage therapists, as well as conscientious, determined business people. We looked for every opportunity to attract new clients while we practiced the passive and active retention techniques with existing clients. We don't have extraordinary super powers; we were merely consistent with our approach to business and persistently attentive in our life goals. You have just as much desire and drive for success as we did when we started. You have all the tools you need to conduct great massages for people, and most likely you have a place where you can perform them. In essence, you have the heart and the hands. And, you have the brain too. When you are feeling like nothing is working out the way you originally planned, don't get down on yourself. Step back and take a deep breath. Look at these principles in all three marketing areas and exercise your brain to create a more successful outcome. There's nothing magic about our personal experience, and there's nothing stopping you from achieving the same kind of success with a little diligence and a lot of work.

By our third year, our growth slowed (as all business growth will do,) but we still did more massages than the year before. We continued to examine our goals and adjust our tactics, but we held true to the belief that if we kept taking care of people's needs on their terms, the business would keep coming to us. All our efforts to get our name into the community from traditional print advertising to networking to pro bono work added up to a recognizable business name throughout our area. People we don't even know are familiar with us, and that does allow us some breathing room in one sense, but it doesn't mean we are resting on our laurels either. We know as soon as we stop marketing our practice we could lose all we've gained. We make new goals, new plans, and we push forward to make them a reality just as we did during those very first months.

In our 4th year, we were so busy we decided to hire employees. Now that's another story all together, and we'll be glad to share that with you later. Our 1st employee alone conducted more massages in ten months (508 massages) than we did together in our first year of business. She became an overnight success because of the foundation we built. Her dream to be a fulltime massage therapist came true without any real effort on her part, but to show up and do massage. The practice, the client, and the paycheck was there waiting for her. We went from 2384 massages in the 3rd year to 3074 massages in the 4th year. By the end of the 7th year, we had 5 fulltime therapists, 3 part-time therapists and 1 fulltime office manager. We had over 7,000 people in our database, 4000± were paying clients. The balance we picked up from free community events and networking. We don't include these numbers to boast about our success, but to give you real numbers, and to show how sticking to these principles do indeed lead to a thriving practice. Reviewing the table (appendix B), you can see where the massages came from and who did them.

We didn't really track where the clients came, although we do ask at the initial intake where they heard about us. Our objective in attracting new clients is a cumulative effort. It's nearly impossible to accurately determine where every single massage comes from based on marketing. A client may have received a free massage at a community event, saw the name of the practice, maybe even took a brochure and read about us, received a note in the mail from us thanking them for the opportunity to work with them, and then looked us up in the yellow pages 9 months later to find out how to book an appointment. That client most likely would write down that they heard about us from the yellow pages because they really couldn't remember the first time they heard about us or remember the number of contacts we directly made with them before the name of our business registered in their mind.

That's why it's so important to be marketing all the time in a variety of ways.

Even if the ink of your certificate is still wet, you can begin utilizing multiple principles to build your business because as soon as you have one client, you can use the principles for retention to ensure they continue to see you as his or her therapist. Likewise, you can examine the relationships you already have for potential opportunities to build Win-Win-Win business relationships. You don't have to have been in business for a long time for any of these principles to work. For those of you who have been beating your heads against the wall about how to achieve a sufficient client base to achieve your goals, you too can employ various principles to make that a reality.

The enviable lifestyle is available to every single practicing massage therapist, as long as you treat your practice as a business. Massage therapy is becoming more and more widely accepted, and that only means more people will be searching for ways in which they can incorporate massage into their lives. You can look out at your community and see the vast potential, or you can flounder aimlessly, wishing and hoping you could some day achieve the success you're after. As with all businesses, action is a necessary requirement for success. It isn't always easy or particularly pleasant in the moment, but consistency and determination always produce positive results.

As you go from here, believe that a sustainable, thriving practice is definitely within your reach. Give yourself credit for the work you do to build your practice. Trust that the seemingly intangible components of doing pro bono work, researching possible target groups, passively retaining your existing clients, or fostering business relationships; will eventually snowball into something tangible. Those things you think aren't currently making you any money right now, and aren't adding value to your bank account, will be the very things that propel your practice into a financially successful practice. We truly believe you can reach and exceed every goal you set your mind to. Your massage practice can be what you dreamed of in massage school and you'll be able to tell yourself; "I'm living my dream." "I have created a successful business and as a result, I am also an experienced, seasoned massage therapist. I've got the best job in the world!"

I have the enviable lifestyle!

Appendix A - Time-Based Marketing Report Card

Time Based Marketing	value system	Monday	Tuesday	Wednesday	Thursday	Friday	Saturday	Sunday	Totals
Free Chair Massage	# x $65								
Follow-up from Chair Massage	# x .50 = $10								
Donated Gift Certificates	# x $65								
Donated Gift Cards	# x $actual								
Handout Personalized Coupons	# x $actual								
Create Advertisements	$10/hr								
Create Coupons	$10/hr								
Visit Group	$65/hr								
Attend Meeting	$65/hr								
Attend Networking Group	$65/hr								
Join Networking Group	actual value								
Refer Business	$10.00								
Speaking Engagement	$100 bonus								
Meet Face to Face	$65/hr								
Display another Business	$10.00								
Volunteer	$50 bonus								
Sign Contract for Work	$10.00								
Write Article	$10.00								
Publish Article	$250 bonus								
Send Thank You Notes	$10/hr								
Make Phone Calls	$10/hr								
Create a New Relationship	$10/hr								
Barter for Advertising	actual value								
Host Reception	$10/hr								
Paid Advertisements	actual value								
Other	actual value								
Total Weekly $$ Credit toward Marketing									
week 1									
week 2									
week 3									
week 4									
Total Monthly $$ Credit									

Appendix B - Yearly Tracking Sheet

	Jan	Feb	Mar	Apr	May	June	July	Aug	Sept	Oct	Nov	Dec	Totals
1st year													
Bill	1	29	22	18	15	19	18	18	20	22	22	25	229
Shelley	2	24	25	19	18	20	12	18	17	27	28	31	241
Totals													470
2nd year													
Bill	43	57	49	73	48	54	57	86	39	79	74	54	713
Shelley	64	66	61	71	57	66	55	81	36	62	62	54	735
pro bono	9	6	1	6	12	14	16	20	27	15	18	12	156
networking	16	22	24	28	22	24	14	11	15	19	13	17	225
3rd year													
Bill	74	88	85	72	98	78	51	82	68	89	90	79	954
Shelley	77	79	91	76	107	88	57	82	80	106	77	82	1002
pro bono	31	20	24	32	32	13	6	3	1	12	13	14	201
networking	13	16	18	23	23	13	19	27	23	27	16	9	227
4th year													
Bill	88	94	92	84	114	70	76	80	33	77	70	71	949
Shelley	91	90	98	98	118	72	80	87	38	88	76	84	1020
employee1	n/a	n/a	13	37	60	51	46	63	58	66	50	58	508
sub	10	8	3	10	5	2	2	0	25	8	4	5	82
pro bono	15	8	10	13	28	5	20	5	36	0	4	5	149
networking	16	30	26	30	20	38	21	37	29	49	44	26	366
Totals													3074

From Our Bookshelf: *Recommended Reading

Books For Improving Your Business Intelligence

The Anatomy of Change, *Richard Strozzi-Heckler*
E-Myth Revisited, *Michael Gerber*
The Art of Exceptional Living, *Jim Rohn*
Instant Advertising, *Bradley J. Sugars*
Instant Cashflow, *Bradley J. Sugars*
Think and Grow Rich, *Napoleon Hill*
Incorporate and Grow Rich, *C.W. Allen*
The Courage to Teach, *Parker J. Palmer*
Screw It, Let's Do It, *Richard Branson*
Rich Dad, Poor Dad, *Robert T. Kiyosaki*
Feel the Fear and Do it Anyway, *Susan Jeffers*
It's a Meaningful Life: It Just Takes Practice, *Bo Lozoff*
What Clients Love, *Harry Beckwith*
Markings, *Dag Hammarskjold*
The Starbuck's Experience: 5 Principles for Turning Ordinary into Extraordinary, *Joseph Michelli*
How to Master the Art of Selling, *Tom Hopkins*
Awake at Work: Facing the Challenges of Life on the Job, *Michael Carroll*
Built to Last: Successful Habits of Visionary Companies, *Jim Collins*

*These books are suggested reading and will, no doubt, become time sensitive with time. We always recommend seeking your own professional, business, marketing, legal, financial and investment advice.

About the Authors

Bill and Shelley sleepwalking through their lives in corporate management jobs, turned 40, and made the conscious decision to change their lives and go back to school to learn massage therapy. They changed careers and opened a massage therapy business called Kneaded Energy®, located in Greensboro, NC. They were "all-in". There was no turning back. What they didn't know about business they found the people they needed for help. They hired a business coach, they hired a personal coach, they downsized their home and living expenses, joined networking groups, read everything they could find about business, found a retired CPA to help them with their budget…and forged ahead until they not only learned enough to become one of the most successful massage therapy businesses in the southeast - but more importantly, until they turned a profit. From this single massage therapy business they have been able to expand and form other lucrative streams of income that compliment their original business.

Bill is originally from Whitesboro, Texas. Bill's background is the food industry. He graduated from the famed Culinary Institute of America in Hyde Park, NY and worked as an executive chef for many years before moving out of the kitchen and into the management of a food services company. His first experience with massage was in combination with psychotherapy and found the two had a profound affect on his life.

Shelley worked in the purchasing, contracts and outsourcing sector of the corporate world. She graduated from Friends University in Wichita, Kansas and began her career at Boeing Airplane Company. She experienced her first massage at the age of 21 and began a conscious lifelong journey to find a way to live in the massage field.

Please Visit our Website: www.EnviableLifestyle.com

Give the Gift of a New, Exciting and Lucrative Massage Therapy Business

Yes, I want _____ copies of <u>**The Enviable Lifestyle, Creating a Successful Massage Therapy Business**</u> at $19.95 each plus $4.00 shipping and handling per book. (North Carolina residents please add appropriate sales tax). Allow 15 days for delivery.

Place your Order by:
Phone: 336-273-1260
Fax:336-273-6221
Web Address:www.EnviableLifestyle.com
Payable by cash, check or credit card (MasterCard, VISA or American Express)

Check out our website for additional materials, books, home-study courses, lecture schedule, videos and revenue generating classes you can teach your clientele.
www.EnviableLifestyle.com

Please Visit our Website: www.EnviableLifestyle.com

Give the Gift of a New, Exciting and Lucrative Massage Therapy Business

Yes, I want _____ copies of **The Enviable Lifestyle: Creating a Successful Massage Therapy Business** at $19.95 each plus $4.00 shipping and handling per book. (North Carolina residents please add appropriate sales tax). Allow 15 days for delivery.

Place your Order by:
Phone: 336-273-1260
Fax:336-273-6221
Web Address:www.EnviableLifestyle.com
Payable by cash, check or credit card (MasterCard, VISA or American Express)
Check out our website for additional materials, books, home-study courses, lecture schedule, videos and revenue generating classes you can teach your clientele.
www.EnviableLifestyle.com

Also Available from www.enviablelifestyle.com

Create Additional Revenue through your Massage Therapy Business Here are simple, how to instructions for teaching massage classes to your clients and the general public. This is a great way to increase the value of your billable hours, subsidize your revenue and educate your clientele about professional, therapeutic massage - making you the expert.

Couples Massage Class Packet $49 plus shipping

The curriculum of this class teaches you how to teach your clients how to work on each other at home. Most massage therapists are skeptical about teaching clients how to do, what you do for them - but the reality is, once they take this class and learn how difficult it can be to deliver a massage - you have just become more valuable in their mind and irreplaceable in their life.

This class packet includes: suggested prices, informed consent, 2 each 8x10 fliers, 25 each brochures, 25 each class handouts, 1 each classroom curriculum and 1 each how to be successful teaching this class to your clients. Additional brochures and handouts are available for $1.00 each plus shipping.

Infant Massage Class Packet $49 plus shipping

The curriculum of this class teaches you how to teach your clients how to work on their newborn babies and toddlers at home. The class introduces the parent to their child in a loving, gentle way at the same time teaching them how to soothe and nourish their baby through touch. This class confirms your position as an authority and professional in the lives of these new parents.

This class packet includes: suggested prices, informed consent, 2 each 8x10 fliers, 25 each brochures, 25 each class handouts (that includes a comprehensive list of "know when to ask for help" instructions), 1 each classroom curriculum and 1 each how to be successful teaching this class to your clients. Additional brochures and handouts are available for $1.00 each plus shipping.

Geriatric Massage Class Packet   **$49 plus shipping**

The curriculum of this class teaches you how to teach your clients how to work on aging parents, relatives and friends. Massage can be such a gentle, relaxing and nourishing way to connect and stay in touch with our aging population - but we all have concerns before we reach out. This class helps to educate about what concerns to look for, when it is ok to touch and when to ask for professional help.

This class packet includes: suggested prices, informed consent, 2 each 8x10 fliers, 25 each brochures, 25 each class handouts (including a comprehensive list of contraindications), 1 each classroom curriculum and 1 each how to be successful teaching this class to your clients. Additional brochures and handouts are available for $1.00 each plus shipping.

Available from www.enviablelifestyle.com